FINISHING THE TASK

*How Indigenous
Missionaries Are
Reaching the Unreached
in the 21st Century*

CHRISTIAN AID MISSION

ISBN 13: 978-1-940545-10-3
ISBN 10: 1-940545-10-3

Thanks to Dr. Bob Finley, the founder of Christian Aid; Cynthia Finley, Raul Hernandez, and John Scully, the Christian Aid Mission staff members who contributed to the creation of this book; and to staff writers Valerie Davis (VD), Joan Hutter (JH), and Brittany Tedesco (BT) who wrote the stories.

CONTENTS

Matthew 24

[4] And Jesus answered and said unto them, Take heed that no man deceive you.

[5] For many shall come in my name, saying, I am Christ; and shall deceive many.

[6] And ye shall hear of wars and rumours of wars: see that ye be not troubled: for all these things must come to pass, but the end is not yet.

[7] For nation shall rise against nation, and kingdom against kingdom: and there shall be famines, and pestilences, and earthquakes, in divers places.

[8] All these are the beginning of sorrows.

[9] Then shall they deliver you up to be afflicted, and shall kill you: and ye shall be hated of all nations for my name's sake.

[10] And then shall many be offended, and shall betray one another, and shall hate one another.

[11] And many false prophets shall rise, and shall deceive many.

[12] And because iniquity shall abound, the love of many shall wax cold.

[13] But he that shall endure unto the end, the same shall be saved.

[14] **And this gospel of the kingdom shall be preached in all the world for a witness unto all nations; and then shall the end come.**

INTRODUCTION

Would it surprise you to learn that $5 could save 10,000 lost souls? In *Finishing the Task,* we document amazing testimonies such as that of Prem Pradhan, a common man who saved people on the streets of Nepal with a $5 Bible. Prem later established a Christian orphanage and raised generations of children who went on to lead thousands upon thousands of people to the Lord.

This compilation of stories celebrates the work of missionaries who impacted their own countries for Christ. Indigenous missionaries preach the gospel in places where traditional missionaries cannot go due to political, cultural, and language barriers. They know the language, they know the people, and they can do the job for a fraction of the cost of a Western missionary. In addition, they can avoid destructive cultural mistakes that plague many missionaries and limit their effectiveness.

Our best guess suggests we have about 7,000 unique nations on this planet, and believers may be found among more than 4,000 of them. According to Mark 13:10 and Matthew 24:14, we may expect our Lord to return when His name is known among all the nations. That's why Christian Aid Mission supports local ministries that plant churches among unreached people groups in more than 3,000 tribes and nations.

Through these inspiring stories, you will discover the eternal impact of native missionaries in our dying world and be encouraged in your Christian walk. It is our hope that after reading these stories you will consider prayerfully partnering with Christian Aid Mission to spread the gospel to the ends of the earth.

NOTE: Although all the stories in this book are true, some of the names have been changed to protect ministries and leaders from hostile authorities and others who might want to harm them.

Christian
Aid
Supporting
Indigenous Ministries

"Unless a grain of wheat falls into the ground and dies, it remains but a single seed."

—John 12:24, ESV

Christian Aid is a pioneer mission that has been helping indigenous missionaries for sixty years. Many of the stories told in this book exemplify the remarkable capacity of men and women of every land to minister to their own people regardless of the cost, while others show the rich history of Christian Aid's impact in the nations. This first story begins in Nepal.

Chapter 1

"I KNOW A MAN WHO DIED AND ROSE AGAIN"

Prem Pradhan took the Bible and told the street preacher he would read it. The preacher had studied with Bahkt Singh, one of India's foremost evangelists.

Born in Nepal, Prem had never heard of Jesus. But because he served in the Indian army, he could freely consider reading the Scriptures. Prem read God's Word twelve times during the next few months.

After praying and giving his life to the Lord, Prem knew God wanted him to return to his own people in the Hindu kingdom of Nepal and tell them about the Man who died and rose again—the Man Jesus Christ.

"But, Lord," Prem said, "I can't. I have a lame leg." He had injured his leg during World War II. How could he trek through the Himalayas?

After three years, Prem surrendered and went home to share his faith. But his family rejected him.

He walked for a year in Nepal over mountains and through forests, fields, and rivers to find one disciple. He slept in barns, on back porch stoops, and under trees in the woods. He ate when someone offered him food.

"I know a Man who died and came to life again," Prem would say to passersby. Not many responded. No one believed.

First Conversions

In the eleventh month of Prem's yearlong journey, he came to the house of a woman who had suffered paralysis for six years. She had spent all she had on the Hindu Lama, but he could not make her walk. Prem told the woman and the Lama, who stood nearby, that he knew someone who could heal her.

> She had spent all she had on the Hindu Lama, but he could not make her walk.

"Who?" the woman asked. "Where is this man?"

"He is right here," Prem replied. He read the Scriptures to the woman, and she asked him to pray for her. Prem prayed in the name of Jesus, pulled her up, and—just as in Acts 3—she began walking, leaping, and praising God. The miracle stunned the handful of witnesses, and they all gave their lives to Jesus.

The Hindu Lama was stunned as well. "By what magic did you cause this woman to walk?" he asked.

"By no magic," Prem answered. "By the power of Jesus Christ."

The Lama believed.

Prem in Prison

In Nepal it is against the law to change one's religion, but Prem openly baptized the new believers in a river where the officials could see. He was committed not to hide the name of Jesus.

The authorities threw them all into prison, sentencing those who were baptized for one year. Prem, who baptized them, was sentenced for six years.

Nine people crowded into a tiny cell with poor ventilation and no sanitation. Each received a cup of rice per day, uncooked, and a cup of water. They slept in the stench on stone floors as rats and lice ate away their clothes.

> They slept in the stench on stone floors as rats and lice ate away their clothes.

During the summer they struggled to survive 100-degree heat; in the winter they nearly froze.

But they had the Scriptures with them, for Prem had read the Bible multiple times as a new believer. He knew the Word by heart and led the prisoners through the Bible from beginning to end three times that year. Those in surrounding cells listened. Prem's first disciples grew up behind bars.

After a year the guards released Prem's friends, but they chained Prem's hands and feet and locked him in a dungeon of corpses. In this dark hole the guards would deposit dead bodies until the family members came to retrieve them. Prem could not stand up. He could not stretch out. The authorities expected him to die or go insane within one week, but Prem sang to Jesus and envisioned the Scriptures. A man truly does not live by bread alone but by the very words of God (see Matthew 4:4), and through the quickening of the Word, Prem survived his ordeal.

Several weeks later, a guard approached the cell and heard talking. He thought Prem would be dead by now. Anyone would.

"Who are you talking to?" the guard yelled into the cell.

"Jesus," Prem answered.

"Who is Jesus?" The guard fetched a torch and shined the light into the cave. "I don't see any Jesus."

"He is here."

Prem shared the gospel with the guard, and he believed.

The guard, who was new on the job, let Prem out of the cell and took him to a nearby well. He gave Prem water and returned him back to the dungeon.

Prem's Witness Spreads

Prem was still alive after spending five months in the corpse chamber. Jesus kept him company and saved his life as people slipped him food. Eventually, the authorities moved Prem to another prison—out of the death hole and into cells with living people.

"I know a Man," he kept saying, "who died and rose again."

Prem was moved again and again—fourteen prisons in ten years—and in each place he spoke of the Lord Jesus. Men from dozens of tribes heard the gospel and believed. When these men were released, they returned to their homes and villages and spread the Word. "There is a

Man who died and rose again," they would say. "His name is Jesus, and He is coming back."

When Prem was released, he did what the Lord showed him to do: He built an orphanage and adopted 100 children. He wanted to raise children to know the Lord Jesus—children who would never have to change their religion and suffer in jail. When those 100 children grew up, many became missionaries.

The price paid early—the seed planted—has produced much fruit today.

Bob Finley's Early Missions Work

Sixty years ago, Bob Finley became convinced that helping indigenous missionaries such as Bahkt Singh in India and Prem in Nepal was the biblical and most effective way to reach the unreached.

As a young man, Finley served as a traditional foreign missionary. He traveled extensively and preached the gospel. Billy Graham backed him during those early days.

But while Finley was ministering in China, he witnessed the door close to foreign missionaries. He saw other doors close in country after country. However, he quickly realized that the believing men and women in those nations were continuing to preach the gospel. They knew the language, culture, and people, and they lived right there among them, sharing in the same lifestyle. They studied the Bible and knew how to pray, because that's what the persecuted church does: prays and fasts.

Prayer Meetings in Korea

One time while visiting Korea, Finley was asked to speak at a 5 A.M. prayer meeting. It was cold, dark, and rainy when he woke up that morning. *No one will be there,* he thought. Nevertheless, he climbed out of bed and trekked through the dark, wet morning to find the meeting. When he arrived, he could not believe his eyes.

Three thousand believers were on their faces, crying out to God.

Three thousand believers were on their faces crying out to God.

There was no preacher or worship leader. One person sang, and all joined in. Another person lifted his voice, and everyone followed. But mostly they all prayed simultaneously, their voices thundering.

"They come every morning," Finley's host said. "We'll have you speak to them in a little while, but keep it short, just to an hour. They have to go to work, and they'll want to pray before that."

Finley spoke for an hour to these souls who were already living the message. His friend told him that believers had prayed daily for sixty years in his country, and this congregation had been coming together faithfully every morning for five years. They took turns, 100 at a time, praying through the night. Many met the Lord at the daybreak meetings, overcome by the supernatural presence of God.

Another time, Finley attended a conference where 3,000 people filled the building and another 10,000 covered the mountainside. The people stayed and prayed all day and night. On the third day, as they continued to praise God through rain and sunshine, they brought in the sick.

When Finley stood to preach, he observed a man lying on the floor in front of him. He thought the man might not make it through the night. He wanted the people to know that even if God didn't heal the man, the important thing to remember was that he would have eternal life.

Just as Finley was about to speak that word—even as the words formed in his mouth—the man stood up and began praising the Lord. The people erupted in praise, and paralytics all over the room stood up and moved their limbs for the first time.

> God was moving in Korea. Finley was changed forever.

God was moving in Korea. Finley was changed forever.

The Emergence of Christian Aid

Finley returned home and dedicated his life to raising funds to help believers in closed, poorer countries preach the gospel to their own people. No Western denominational ties were needed. Finley just wanted to help them by sending funds to qualified ministries.

As Finley traveled and preached in the United States, he told these two stories—of Prem in Nepal and of the worshipping believers in Korea. From these stories—and others like them—Christian Aid emerged. These experiences inspired Finley and Christian Aid to help pioneer the paradigm shift in foreign missions toward supporting indigenous missions. Through the years, others have followed.

Today, Christian Aid helps 80,000 indigenous missionaries move forward with the gospel. Missions the indigenous way—ministries in their own lands spreading the gospel to their own people—will finish the task of planting a witness for Christ in every nation. These ministries have the heart and heed the call. With help from believers in prosperous countries, they will ensure that every kindred, tongue, people, and nation has a witness for Christ Jesus. They will reach the last unreached peoples of the earth, and then the end will come.

—JH

Discover More!

Go online to www.christianaid.org/ftt/1 and check out the Christian Aid world Map.

NEXT STORY ...

"One generation shall praise thy works to another, and shall declare thy mighty acts."

—*Psalm 145:4*

Prem's prison cell reeked with dead bodies. The biblical Daniel's prison den quaked with lions. Both knew the powerful presence of the Lord. God shut the mouths of the lions for Daniel and gave Prem a song of praise to sustain him.

The Lord's presence also upholds the next generation.

Gagan Bahadur, who grew up in Prem's orphanage, was the youngest of seven children. He followed in the steps of an older brother, who had given his life to Jesus. Bahadur's parents put them both out of the house, thinking they would displease their Hindu gods. Bahadur's older brother could not afford to feed him, so when he heard about Prem's home and school, he knew he'd found the place for Bahadur.

Bahadur gained an education and a heart for Jesus. He graduated and set out to plant a church, and later he continued his education in Bible school and theological training outside the country. He returned to Nepal some years later with his new wife, Sunita, whom he met while studying the Scriptures. The two shared a passion for the lost and made a phenomenal ministry team. They have since planted 186 churches with 10,000 members in Nepal and built five orphanages that care for more than 500 children.

Prem declared the mighty acts of God to Bahadur, and now the Bahadurs do the same for the next generation through their ministry.

But reaching the unreached in Nepal still calls for courage.

The following chapter offers a glimpse of what it takes to reach just one remote mountain tribe in this country. Persecution?

Yes. Sometimes, angry villagers throw stones at Bahadur and his missionary team. Beatings? Yes. Even as a youth at Prem's orphanage and school, Bahadur experienced violence. He also witnessed killings when the authorities shut down the school for a time, rejecting what they perceived as Western religion.

But this chapter deals more with the risks of traveling with the gospel. Who would traverse jungles and climb steep mountains for days to reach a naked, destitute people on a mountaintop? Who would face tigers, cobras, leeches, and thieves to bring the gospel to the next people group—to plant a witness for Christ among them?

Gagan Bahadur does this to the glory of God.

He may not suffer death-dungeons or lions' dens, but he journeys through beastly jungles.

Chapter 2

LEECHES, TIGERS, AND STAMPEDING ELEPHANTS

Gagan Bahadur—the leader of a church-planting ministry of 186 churches that includes a training center, Bible school, and five orphanages—lives by another voice.

The Lord's calling propels him to engage every village with the gospel, regardless of the cost. Wild animals cannot hold him back. Nor can any other danger lurking in the jungles of Nepal.

Monkeys scream for the flour and spices in his pack. They can have them.

A cobra coils around his legs. He'll live.

Trudging through jungles and over mountains takes days. His life is often threatened deep in the tangles. But he always reaches his destination.

Blood-sucking leeches gather in droves. When missionaries step into a swamp, the 10-inch leeches attach themselves onto their bodies. Half-inchers hang from trees, smelling the human presence, and drop onto their

> When missionaries step into a swamp, the 10-inch leeches attach themselves onto their bodies.

heads. They slither up from the ground, nearly invisible, and go undetected for hours.

"We face these experiences all the time traveling on foot," says Bahadur. Welcome to the world of an indigenous pioneer missionary who is passionate about *finishing the task*. He *must* plant a witness for Christ where no one dare endeavor.

Caught in a Flood

Other threats loom. In the mountains, where rains pound the earth, rivers swiftly rise. Fierce currents uproot trees and trigger landslides. Bahadur recalls traveling alone one time in eastern Nepal when a flood suddenly flashed, its waters covering his shoulders and neck.

"Help!" he shouted again and again. But no one came. He grasped tightly his Bible and hymnbook in one hand while desperately reaching through the rapids for a branch that would hold him. But he found none.

"I was feeling dizzy because the water was flowing so strongly," Bahadur said.

Nearly half an hour passed as he struggled for life. Then, as the water lashed his face, a huge tree swept down the river and pierced him through the side, carrying him more than four miles.

"It was painful. I was bleeding, but at the same time I realized God was sending this tree to save me," Bahadur said. "I was so thankful to God, though it was scary and I was in desperate need. I was thankful to the Lord for the way the tree came and saved me and took me away."

Some ways down the rolling river, the tree caught on a larger tree and brought Bahadur to a halt. Gradually, the flood subsided. Bahadur had survived.

He pulled himself free from the piercing branch. As he began to make his way across the river, people from the next village came to help him. They held hands and made a human chain.

Bahadur's books and clothes sagged with mud and water. He felt weak and cold, but his heart overflowed with the mercy of God. The people carried him to their village and fed him. After a meal of pigeon soup, he traveled on that same day until he reached the mountaintop, where a revival meeting awaited him.

"That night we had a fellowship, and many people committed their lives to the Lord," he recalls. "Even that wet Bible and hymnbook were useful. They wanted to dry them in the sunshine and use them."

Whether leeches or floods, these trials mark the trails of evangelistic missionaries who persevere through fear and never give up. The God of Wonders gives them wisdom in the moment.

> These trials mark the trails of evangelistic missionaries who persevere through fear and never give up.

Facing Down a Tiger

"I faced a tiger," Bahadur says.

He was bounding down a mountain one day when he landed just three feet above the wild cat. He winced. The tiger was hovering over a goat and drinking blood from its neck. When Bahadur landed, the tiger jerked and looked up at him.

For what seemed like twenty minutes, they stared at each other—eye to eye. Neither budged. Bahadur felt the fear swell in the back of his throat. Sweat beaded on his brow, and his heart raced.

Finally, a rush of adrenalin burst through him, and he roared with all his might. To his amazement the tiger bolted to an opening in the field two dozen meters ahead.

Bahadur roared again, and the tiger leapt to a lower terrace and glared back at him. Another shout, and the tiger dashed out of sight. Bahadur put the goat on his back and ran nearly five miles to a small community of houses.

God had opened his mouth with a roar—and closed the mouth of the tiger.

> God had opened his mouth with a roar—and closed the mouth of the tiger.

The goat became a meal for those people. Although Bahadur was too weak to eat or speak for three days, he was soon journeying again. The gospel keeps going.

"That's how we do it all the time," he says. "You have to be very careful when you walk."

Threats and Stampeding Elephants

Bahadur abounds with stories of survival.

Friends say, "Don't go; it's too risky." Tigers, wild elephants, and thieves pepper the path. But Bahadur knows the Lord leads him—even if it is through the valley of the shadow of death (see Psalm 23:4). He travelled with Prem Pradhan, his spiritual father, and now he recognizes it's his turn to carry the torch.

After all, if not Bahadur, who will proclaim the good news on the mountains?

No moon gave light the night he and three others took sticks for protection and set out through the wilderness to minister at a distant village. Every shadow rose like a mountain over the brave travelers.

"It was scary, but we wanted to go to the fellowship that night," Bahadur says. "There is no transportation at night, because people are afraid to drive there."

Halfway to the village, they heard voices of men hurling threats at them. So they hid in some roadside bushes. When the mutters faded, the team moved on, but then the ground rumbled with the clamor of elephants. Bahadur and his band shouted and threw stones to deter them.

Meanwhile, with just one flashlight, they ran two hours through the black night until they reached their destination—a gathering of leaders.

"I think the Lord really wanted us to go and help them," Bahadur says, "and also hear what the Lord was doing through them."

The believers described receiving harsh imprisonments for their faith. Some of the women lived alone because their husbands still suffered behind bars. But the women rejoiced anyway.

"Don't worry about us," they said. "We are here for the sake of our faith. We even have the privilege of sharing the gospel among prisoners."

On a hidden mountainside, these saints live for the Great Commission.

Worth the Cost

"Sometimes you walk four, five, or six days to reach a village," Bahadur says. "Just to climb one steep mountain can take five or six hours—after crossing so many jungles, rivers, and small hills—just to reach the top where the churches are established. It is not an easy road."

But it is worth it.

"When we see people come to Jesus, it is really joyful," Bahadur says. "The pain and difficulties—whatever we face on the way—can't compare. It is wonderful to be mightily used by God for those simple people in the mountains. They thank God because their sins are forgiven and they are set free."

Bahadur says that this is what the Lord is doing on the mountains. "Many Christians don't even know what is happening on the top of the mountain because they can't go there. So we are committed to those areas, to reach out with the gospel and motivate those few believers who already are converted to reach out to others."

Bahadur says his family tells him not to go. "Why don't you send other people?" they ask. He replies, "Well, if we risk their lives, why do we not risk our own?"

> "Well, if we risk their lives, why do we not risk our own?"

Landslides, floods, beasts ... so many risks. But these missionaries never give up preaching Christ. They possess zeal, vision, and courage because they believe they are called to be God's instruments. They go to every village, crossing many mountains and valleys to knock on doors and tell people about Jesus.

"Even with all these difficulties, we have decided to go wherever the door is open," Bahadur says.

These brave men and women follow the voice of the Lord—"the voice of one calling in the wilderness: 'Prepare the way of the Lord'" (Mark 1:3, ESV).

—JH

Discover More!

Get current news on indigenous missions groups around the globe.

www.christianaid.org/ftt/2

NEXT STORY ...

"When he saw the multitudes, he was moved with compassion on them, because they fainted, and were scattered abroad, as sheep having no shepherd."

—*Matthew 9:36*

When a man follows Jesus, he learns His heart.

Prem and Bahadur followed the Lord into prisons and through the jungles of Nepal. Compelled by the Holy Spirit, they experienced His sustaining presence.

The God of all compassion never leaves us or forsakes us. The ever-present One knows the needs of the helpless.

With compassion, Jesus became flesh and dwelt among His people (see John 1:14). With compassion, His ministers care for the lost. And with compassion, the ones He calls reach the poor and needy.

Here begins the story of PJ Thomas (1915–1998)—India's Man of Compassion—who considered thousands of homeless children his own to feed. He pioneered a training center that prepared 3,000 indigenous missionaries for the lost sheep of India. He also chartered the first women's Bible college in that country so women could carry the gospel to other women.

He couldn't look away from those who were suffering. He couldn't harden his heart.

INDIA

Chapter 3

INDIA'S MAN OF COMPASSION

Painummoottil John (PJ) Thomas, a second-generation Christian, felt a pang in his spirit as he gazed out over the sea of filthy children. Everywhere, roaming youngsters with twig-like legs and distended tummies filled the roads, their bony arms twisted from sagging shoulders. Hollow eyes told the story of abandonment or hopelessness. Listless stares broadcasted empty bowls and cupboards, if indeed they had a home.

The children trotted along behind oxcarts and scooped up manure to take home for cooking fuel. Older boys pushed and shoved to harvest the precious droppings, leaving the smaller children with empty bags.

One boy was so hungry he slipped under a fence and picked a small sweet potato from a field. The farmer broke his fingers. But Thomas took him in.

Thomas tucked dozens of other starving street boys under his arms and carried them home.

He gave chickens, eggs, and baby goats to poor children. The chickens produced about an egg a day, and with patience provided another chicken—and more eggs to eat or harvest. The milk from goats filled the bellies of babes.

With 100 million children under the age of fifteen in India, most fall among the poorest of the poor.

"I have 2 million within my immediate reach," Thomas said. "The women of our fellowship cook an extra handful of rice for their neighbors."

But even this was a drop in the bucket.

"Someday," Thomas said, "I would like to be known as the Father of 10,000 Children."

Sermon on the Mount Ministry

During his life, PJ Thomas lived as India's "Man of Compassion." His heart beat for children. But he also trained young people for the mission field.

From a young age Thomas held dear the faith-walk of Sadhu Sundar Singh, the man of God who dedicated him as a child. Singh depended on God. So would Thomas.

Thomas held degrees from four universities and Bible institutes, but he decided he didn't need a diploma to prove His ability to teach, preach, and show compassion. He imprinted on his name card, "Crossing the sea does not make one a missionary; seeing the cross does." He discarded his special letters and diplomas.

In 1952, Thomas and his wife, Aleyamma, bought an old house in the center of Tiruvalla on low-lying ground. The water lilies reminded him of the "rose of Sharon" in the Bible (Song of Solomon 2:1), so he named his work Sharon Fellowship.

Thousands of Indians lacked the means to attend Bible school. So, steeped in the Lord's Sermon on the Mount message, Thomas opened his doors to a unique school where young men came and went as needed. He decided that if the Lord Jesus taught this way standing on the mountain as crowds ebbed and flowed, so could he.

Thomas began the Bible institute in his living room. With no

16

exams and no degree, the students trusted the Lord to confirm their call. "We don't need to examine our food in order to digest it," Thomas said.

Nine students came the first year. Soon there were twenty. From his own supply, Thomas paid for study materials and food. He knew the young men had nothing and wouldn't come if they had to pay.

He trusted the Lord for provision. But one day his cash ran out. They had eaten the last grains of rice.

So they waited on the Lord. Gathering for 5 a.m. devotions, Thomas read of the manna that fell from heaven. They prayed for a miracle, and they felt the Scripture reading came directly from the Lord. They worshipped the God who brought water from a rock in the wilderness and rained down manna from heaven.

When the students went outside that morning, they shouted with joy. Bushels of edible mushrooms had sprung up throughout the grounds. Never again did they appear so abundantly. The experience showed Thomas and the students that they served the living God—the God of all compassion who was aware of every need.

Supply from America

In 1972, Thomas visited America and met Bob Finley, founder of Christian Aid. Finley had just received $40 for his personal needs from a friend, but when he heard the story of pioneer missionaries living by faith, he gave Thomas half of what he had.

"We'll see what God can do," he said.

Finley sent out a letter expressing the needs of Sharon Fellowship, and the funds began to come in. Over the years American donors sent thousands of dollars to support the Bible school, missionaries, and needy children.

Bible Women

Upon returning to India, Thomas' wife met him with another challenge.

"There are 400 million women in India," she said. "In our culture, men dare not speak with them, only women. We need a Bible institute for women."

So Thomas and Aleyamma started India's first Bible college for women and trained hundreds of women in the Word of God. Later, with help, Sharon Fellowship built dorms for both men and women, training thousands to reach India for Christ.

As part of their training, the Bible women visited women and children in homes, encouraging them and sharing the gospel of Jesus. Like arrows, the women's Bible institute pierced the hearts of many families and homes. Testimonies of miracles rose like beacons of light among these quiet servants.

One time, an elderly Hindu woman with cancer came to a women's outreach. When the women prayed for her, the cancer left her body. Through this healing, she came to believe in Christ Jesus and received Him as her Lord and Savior.

Later, when the woman tried to attend the meetings, her relatives tied her up so she couldn't leave the house. They did this repeatedly. Once as she prayed while tightly bound, she saw a flashing light. An angel of the Lord appeared and loosed her, as an angel had done for Peter in Acts 12.

Through Thomas' ministry, many women saw the spiritual chains fall from their lives as they studied God's Word.

Army of Common People

Thomas trained lay evangelists who carried the gospel to unreached villages and tribes that had never heard the name of Jesus. He called these evangelists God's "advance men." They were forerunners of the faith who forged a path for the gospel.

"We have an army of common people," Thomas said. "They are not ordained ministers, but they are soul winners. During Hindu festival days, they go barefoot to the temples where hundreds of thousands of Hindus flock to bow down before images. Our people stand under bamboo and

> "We have an army of common people," Thomas said. "They are not ordained ministers, but they are soul winners."

mango trees. They set up a picture of the crucifixion and preach to the common people."

Thomas said that his people would distribute gospel tracts printed on a crude printing machine. "They give out millions of tracts during a one-week Hindu *mela,* or festival. Then we receive letters from Hindus wanting to know more about the Lord Jesus. They just don't understand how one man can take away the sin of many people. So we explain the gospel message."

During the 1980s, about 300 men served the Lord as full-time missionaries with Sharon Fellowship. Another 300 ladies served as Bible women. The army of lay preachers—2,000 strong after a decade—completed the ranks of Sharon's vast ministry. Together they established more than 300 churches and mission stations in India.

When these lay missionaries went out, they resigned from their jobs and left their homes to preach the gospel. Their empty stomachs hoped for a meal along the way. Their blistered feet longed for sandals. But an urgency to share the One who had set them free compelled them. Kicked and beaten, they pressed on in the strength of Christ.

These men and women did more than any outsider could do—and the numbers have impacted India's lost millions.

"Give us the tools and we will do the job," Thomas said, "because our people know the customs and the manners. India is a mass of people. Convert one today, another tomorrow, and we will make an impact."

"Give us the tools and we will do the job."

Following this principle, Thomas trained more than 3,000 native missionaries during his lifetime, who won more than 30,000 souls to Christ. He also found support for hundreds of pioneer missionaries.

Acts of compassion still remain at the heart of this ministry. Yet as far as the missionaries take the gospel, their hearts begin and end on the streets with the children.

A Legacy of Compassion

During Thomas' life, Sharon Fellowship's 3,000 missionaries served with dozens of mission works all over India. They cared for more than 100 orphans and delivered food to thousands of other needy children through the "Chickens for Children" and "Kids [baby goats] for Kids" programs.

"A chicken for every child and an egg every Sunday," Thomas would say. Through the gift of a chicken, Sharon Fellowship provided for impoverished children wandering the streets of India. "We give the unwanted children in the street free chickens, and every Sunday each one brings an egg to us. These we distribute to the poorer children."

Thomas couldn't ignore the children. He placed 100 in an orphanage, and hundreds more went to live in Christian homes. He fed and ministered to thousands more in the crowded streets of India. Indeed, he became the "Father of 10,000 Children" and "India's Man of Compassion."

Now Sharon Fellowship carries the baton of the pioneer Thomas to impact another generation of children and gospel workers, both men and women. And all for the glory of the Lord.

—JH

Discover More!

Want to inspire your children to be a part of advancing the kingdom of God? Check out Prayerline for Kids online.

www.christianaid.org/ftt/3

NEXT STORY ...

"Love never fails."

—*1 Corinthians 13:8, NKJV*

Gabriel Barau has always viewed his work among the unreached people groups in Nigeria as a battle between God's people and the forces of evil. Those forces have taken many forms, but perhaps none so menacing as Boko Haram—the very name of which strikes fear into the hearts of Nigerians. These terrorists have murdered thousands in their attempt to stamp out any who might oppose Islam's brutal conquest of Nigeria.

Yet while many in Nigeria run from their society's most feared and hated members, Barau and his coworkers run toward them. And they have won several to Christ through their powerful demonstration of His love.

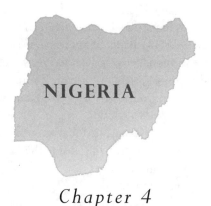

NIGERIA

Chapter 4

THE BATTLE FOR UNREACHED PEOPLE

As the sun began to set, Gabriel Barau took a seat on the ground among the naked villagers. The beast roasting over the fire was a rare departure from the tribe's usual fare of grubs, as evidenced by the hair still clinging to the carcass. Barau, the man of the hour, was handed the first chunk of unskinned goat. He bit into the leathery mass. For him, it was merely another step in the arduous process of being accepted into the tribe.

Only months earlier, Barau had learned that this tribe, called Koma, had been accidentally rediscovered after being hidden from society for more than 100 years. He set off for Koma Hills, the remote mountain range bordering Cameroon, and found the tribe for himself in June 1983. Following in the footsteps of the apostle Paul, Barau determined to become "all things to all men" (1 Corinthians 9:22). He lived among them and adopted their primitive way of life. Eventually, he earned the right to speak into their lives.

Overwhelmed by Barau's extraordinary gesture, the tribe had thrown him a celebration. Still gnawing on the first gristly bite of goat, Barau stood to greet the approaching village chief. To fully express his appreciation, the chief offered Barau an extra special gift—an intimate evening with his wife.

Barau declined.

The chief still remained friends with him, however, and heartily accepted the improvements that Barau offered to bring to his people. Using the Bible as a textbook, Barau began teaching adult literacy classes, which proved an enormous success. Gathering the children together, Barau also started a primary school, initially conducted underneath a tree. Years later, with help from Christian Aid, Barau was able to open a secondary school and a medical clinic.

By 1989, the first-ever Koma missionaries were evangelizing their own people. The Spirit of Christ, living inside the Koma believers, had a curious effect on their community. Although they maintained their cultural identity, they began to reject certain practices that no longer had a place in the life of a Christ follower. The Word of God, applied to their lives, brought dignity and respect— elevating them to an entirely new status.

> The Spirit of Christ, living inside the Koma believers, had a curious effect on their community.

In 2005, the first Koma doctor graduated from medical school. Today, more than forty Koma churches stand as symbols of God's power, working through one submitted individual, to transform entire communities.

Early Days

Not content to rest after reaching the Koma tribe, Barau and a few missionary coworkers set out in search of other lost people. Calling themselves Missionary Crusaders Ministries (MCM), they entered a village inhabited by the Dirim people.

Much to their surprise, they discovered that Methodist and Lutheran churches had been established there, but without any viable results. The Dirim still practiced witchcraft and made animal sacrifices to an idol named Kamage. The villagers would remove their shirts and shoes and bow before its image.

As Barau and his coworkers walked through the Dirim communities and spoke with the people, they discovered one particular village open to the gospel. Could Barau provide them with a simple shelter to act as a meeting place for discipleship? He calculated that only $300 would be needed to meet this modest request.

But these were the early days. The ministry had no money, and Christian Aid had only just begun to raise funds for them. Yet Barau knew that to the poor tribal villagers, the simple church would be more than just a shelter from the elements. It would demonstrate God's care for them and legitimize their faith to the rest of the community. So Barau began to raise the necessary funds to build the church.

Two long years later, Barau returned with the money he had diligently saved from the meager gifts of poor believers. But he was too late. Muslims, offering material aid, had already infiltrated the village and converted everyone.

The Battle

The difficult Dirim experience taught Barau an important truth. "Possessing the unreached people for the Lord is a battle between God's people and the kingdom of darkness," he wrote in a letter to Christian Aid. He became more aware of this battle that was silently raging around him and of the enemy who was

> "Possessing the unreached people for the Lord is a battle between God's people and the kingdom of darkness."

diligently watching him, studying him for weakness. To rescue people entrapped in this enemy's camp, he needed to do more than just show up. He needed a strategy.

So, before Barau approached the next unreached people group, he first studied the tribe. He assessed their unique culture, customs, and beliefs. He analyzed potential obstacles to their acceptance of Christ. His research enabled him to contextualize, or make relevant, the gospel for a particular ethnicity.

Barau prepared as much as possible. Knowing that financial resources would be a continual challenge, he focused on what he did have: people. He poured time into his coworkers, training and discipling them to be effective witnesses for Christ. "The call of God is not just to make converts, but to make disciples," he said. Barau's rigorous program produced an army of spiritually mature graduates who were biblically grounded and fully equipped for the difficult work ahead of them on the mission field.

Ministry Among the Verre

Barau sent one graduate, Ifeanyi, to move with his wife into a simple mud hut in Verre territory. The Verre are an Islamic and animistic tribe of more than 100,000 who live in Nigeria's Muslim-dominated Northeast. Largely a vast plain, the Verre field is also comprised of outlying mountain communities. Without transportation, Ifeanyi had to walk for days through the huge region to reach scattered villages.

One evening at twilight, after spending a few days ministering in the mountains, Ifeanyi descended the steep wilds. A troop of baboons, vicious animals known to kill humans, surrounded him. He ran for his life and ended up twisting his knee and tearing his ligaments.

> A troop of baboons, vicious animals known to kill humans, surrounded him.

Although expensive medical treatment was beyond MCM's means at the time, Christian Aid sent $1,000 to provide Ifeanyi with a motorcycle. Now, villages that had taken him three days to reach on foot took only a few hours.

Ifeanyi continued ministering for the next eight years until, at the age of thirty-five, he could no longer walk. With gifts from Christian Aid donors—who were by then well acquainted with MCM—Ifeanyi was sent to India for knee surgery. Back in action, he now supervises six key MCM mission fields.

Ministry Among the Fulani

With more than 170 million people, Nigeria is Africa's most populous nation. The country's 500-plus people groups are sharply divided between the feudalistic Islamic North and the entrepreneurial Christian South. In 1993, Barau chose to rent an office in Yola, an Islamic city in the North, to serve as his ministry's headquarters.

After all, it was in the North that he and his coworkers could better reach the Fulani. This unreached people group, who wander the vast deserts and savannahs of West and Central Africa, represent the largest nomadic tribe in the world. Between 15 and 20 million Fulani live in

Nigeria alone. Highly resistant to outsiders, mission work among this Sunni Muslim tribe is extremely dangerous.

Barau, knowing that all of West Africa would be affected if he could reach this group, began formulating ways to contextualize the gospel for the Fulani. In 2002, MCM sent missionaries to strategic stopping places where Fulani travelers trade and pick up needed supplies. Gradually, they formed relationships.

> All of West Africa would be affected if he could reach this group.

Barau learned one important fact about the Fulani: they value their cattle above all else. As herdsmen controlling 90 percent of the nation's cattle, the Fulani devote their lives to their cows. Their children go uneducated, as they too are required to spend their days herding cattle.

Barau realized that if he could reach the children by educating them in the evenings, he had a chance of reaching the adults. He envisioned a mobile school that would follow this nomadic people. He prayed for a breakthrough.

This breakthrough came in the form of a Fulani man named Ardo. One day as he was herding his beloved cattle across a farmer's property, the animals decimated the crops. Ardo expected a violent fight when the owner of the crops approached him. But the farmer, who happened to be an MCM missionary, was gracious and loving. He led Ardo and his entire family to Christ.

Ardo's tribal elders commanded him to recant his faith. When he refused, they falsely accused him of stealing and imprisoned him for three years. During this time, Ardo, his wife, and his children were tortured and threatened. To force his denial of Christ, the tribal leaders fatally poisoned three of his children.

In spite of the ordeal, Ardo stood for the Lord. He has since joined MCM, evangelizing groups of nomads. His powerful

> To force his denial of Christ, the tribal leaders fatally poisoned three of his children.

testimony won the hearts of several Fulani who expressed their desire for a church building, which Christian Aid provided in 2007. Ardo continues to use the building as a discipleship center to shelter new converts while they mature in their faith.

In 2009, Christian Aid brought to life Barau's original vision for a mobile school to follow the Fulani. The funds Barau received enabled him to purchase a vehicle and fill it with educational materials. Barau also purchased medical supplies (for humans and cattle), Fulani Bibles, cots, a generator, and a video projector for Christian films. The work exploded. Fulani chiefs soon began welcoming Barau into their villages to accept his help and listen to his message.

The Battle Rages On

That same year, as MCM effectively used its new "school on wheels" to claim souls for Christ formerly in Satan's grasp, the forces of hell broke loose in Adamawa State, the home of MCM's headquarters. A group of Islamic extremists, who called themselves Boko Haram, began a bloody rampage to establish Sharia law throughout the country.

As of the writing of this book, Boko Haram has killed more than 5,000 men, women, and children. Thousands more have been maimed and wounded. The group's original targets were schools and police stations, but they have since focused on Christians. Today, Boko Haram members wait outside of churches and open fire on believers as they exit Sunday services.

Several MCM workers stationed at their mission fields lost their homes when Boko Haram set fire to them. The school on wheels became a life-saving escape vehicle, as MCM used it to evacuate missionaries and converts from two fields where Boko Haram had invaded and killed more than 400 people.

"Every day we live with the threat of death for ourselves and our children," Barau says.

Though active throughout the entire North, Boko Haram has concentrated its assault on Adamawa State. This barrage of attacks compelled Barau to

> "Every day we live with the threat of death for ourselves and our children."

move his headquarters. With help from Christian Aid, he has almost finished construction on a new building in a safer location. However, the ministry still maintains a presence in the North.

Many missionaries are determined to stay in their fields, refusing to leave behind those whom they are reaching.

These missionaries' faithful efforts paid off in 2013, when three Boko Haram members gave their lives to Christ. Barau worked quickly to move them and their families to a remote plot of land that had previously been provided by Christian Aid to serve as a safe haven for Fulani believers rejected by their communities. The move was not made quickly enough, however, for one of the former terrorists. Angry Boko Haram radicals learned of his faith and murdered his wife and children.

Moving Forward

While the battle for lost souls rages on, Barau knows that God will ultimately triumph. This keeps him moving forward. Terrorists may have invaded his nation and hindered his work, but he will never stop.

As Barau now prepares to reach two new people groups, he pauses to celebrate thirty years of ministry since those early days on Koma Hills. He is grateful to the Lord for enabling him to share Christ with seventeen unreached tribes, including the Dirim people. Not only has MCM taken back the village converted by Muslims when Barau struggled to raise funds for a church, but the ministry has also planted five additional churches throughout Dirim territory.

—BT

Discover More!

Watch the video "Just Imagine" online to discover the effectiveness of indigenous missions.

www.christianaid.org/ftt/4

NEXT STORY ...

"To live is Christ, and to die is gain."

—*Philippians 1:21*

In the Philippines, a group as equally disdained as Nigeria's Boko Haram inhabits many of the islands in the archipelago. Cannibals live in the heart of those virgin jungles. And while civilized society fears and avoids them, one native ministry leader, Bayani Leyson, seeks after them.

Their savagery does not concern him, for he is focused on their eternal souls. Through his courage, he has brought many of them into the Kingdom of God. Now, instead of killing people, they are loving them. Leyson is willing to do whatever it takes to build God's Kingdom—even if it takes his life.

PHILIPPINES

Chapter 5

WHATEVER IT TAKES

Bayani Leyson's motorcycle only takes him so far through the thick jungles of Davao del Norte before he must dismount and journey on foot. The route is perilous, but as he travels he has one thing on his mind—and it is not his personal safety. Leyson is concerned only for the eternal souls of those forgotten or feared by society who live like wild animals amid the tangle of trees.

En route to a jungle tribe, Leyson approaches the concealed camp-grounds of the communist New People's Army. He stops to retrieve a few bottles of amoxicillin from his pocket and hand them to a man who appears to be the leader of the camp. It is always a good idea to have a gift for them—those who come empty-handed are never treated kindly.

The camp leader inspects the bottles suspiciously and then looks up. His eyes slowly scan Leyson's face for some crack in the façade—one hint of questionable intent will earn Leyson an extended stay at the camp. Reluctantly, the leader steps aside for Leyson to pass.

Leyson pushes back the leaves of the dense foliage, knowing that he is getting closer to his destination. The sound of voices can now be heard. He slows his stride in an attempt to mask the sound of his footsteps, but a branch snaps under his foot. The voices suddenly stop.

Almost instantly, a few of the scariest-looking humans he has ever seen surround him. Leyson looks into the eyes of these men—crazed and vicious—and then to the spears in their hands, and then to their animal-skin coverings that are stained with

> A few of the scariest-looking humans he has ever seen surround him.

blood. The stench tells him that baths are long overdue. He requests to be taken to their chief. He has good news to share.

Living on the Edge

Only later does Leyson discover that he has shared Christ with one of the Aeta tribes, a fierce group who hunt with bows and arrows and are known to prove their bravery by killing and eating the livers of their enemies.

Sharing Christ with unreached people groups in the Philippines is no easy task. The 7,000 islands are home to 190 ethnic groups that speak 77 dialects. Leyson and his wife speak five.

Leyson and his team of native missionaries never know who or what awaits them when they set off in boats toward remote islands. The tribes inhabiting many of those islands do not take kindly to outsiders. The Magindanaw tribe, who live in Mindanao alongside the Abu Sayyaf terrorist group and constitute the largest group of Muslim Filipinos, killed one believer who worked with Leyson's ministry. The murder was meant to keep Christians away, but it only served to pique Leyson's interest.

On his second visit to the tribe, he brought a generator, a projector, and a screen to show a gospel film. More than 200 curious tribal Muslims attended, including ten imams. That night an underground church was born among those who had given their lives to Christ. Translation of the Bible into the Maguindanao language soon began.

Another violent tribe in the region, the Ilongot, still practice head-hunting. Several years after Leyson planted churches among them, he was invited to a meeting of eighteen Ilongot pastors. As they prayed and spoke excitedly about the work God was doing among their people,

Leyson's attention was fixed on their ears, most of which were scarred with one or two large holes.

Leyson later learned that the number of holes in an Ilongot man's ears symbolizes the number of men he has decapitated. These men, who had once sought to kill their enemies, were now loving them through the transforming power of Christ in their lives.

> The number of holes in an Ilongot man's ears symbolizes the number of men he has decapitated.

Early Life

Leyson grew up under the guidance of his father, Gani, who in 1970 established a church in Mindanao. A challenging mission field, Mindanao is in economic and moral decay. Unemployment is rampant, and foreign investors have fled for fear of being abducted for ransom payments by Islamic terrorists.

Leyson gave his heart to Christ at an early age. He soon began helping his father in ministry by assisting in evangelistic meetings, where he operated the film projector, led worship, and even preached. In 1979, Gani established a Bible college with support from Christian Aid for those church members who expressed a desire to evangelize their communities. The students were taught not just to make converts but to also make disciples. Practically, this meant establishing churches that functioned as schools to educate and train children in the knowledge of God's Word. Students who graduated from the Bible college were expected to become both pastors and principals.

The challenges faced by the graduates included more than just lack of sleep. In 1994, a graduate named Estigoy Dakila established a church, school, and Bible college. Four years later, hostile Muslim neighbors ransacked the church. The students returned from an educational field trip to find their rice, clothing, bedding, books, and Bibles scattered everywhere. The building was partially demolished. For the next six months—until funds could be raised locally to rebuild—the students slept on benches inside the crumbled walls of the church.

More Than Status Quo

As a teenager, Leyson watched this same scenario unfold in the lives of the gospel workers under his father's supervision. These workers were persecuted and threatened and often struggled to feed their families. Sometimes they became discouraged at their seeming lack of progress. When Leyson neared his high school graduation, he determined to avoid the hardship of life in the ministry.

Leyson completed his education in 1993 and chose a safe, predictable job as an airplane mechanic. The stability was comfortable … at first. But as Leyson recalled the danger, risk, and adventure in the lives of the evangelists trained by his father, his job became monotonous at best. After one year as a mechanic, he enrolled in his father's Bible college. It was there he met his wife.

After attending Bible college, Leyson moved to a small rented house on the relatively affluent island of Luzon, where he established a church. During the next six years, Leyson and his wife had three children. They started four additional churches and a Bible school with help from Christian Aid.

Life was good. The churches were doing well, and sixty students were being groomed in the Bible school for ministry. The church members in Luzon were able to tithe regularly, and Leyson's family never went hungry. However, the region of Mindanao remained in Leyson's heart, and he felt the tug to return. Several prominent cults had infiltrated the region, and its adherents were unashamedly preaching their blasphemous views in the city streets.

"I observed that these cults, who were preaching against Jesus as the Son of God, were very brave," Leyson said. "I figured that I, knowing the Truth, should be equally as bold."

> "I observed that these cults, who were preaching against Jesus as the Son of God, were very brave."

Leaving Luzon

In 1999, Leyson chose a trusted gospel worker to lead his ministry in Luzon and moved his family to Mindanao to begin an evangelistic ministry. He stood in public markets, parks, shopping malls, and bus terminals to preach the message of Christ to anyone who would listen. Sometimes, angry Muslims confronted him. Sometimes, those same Muslims stopped to listen.

Money was tight, but God always provided for Leyson and his family. Passersby often left him with small bundles of fruit or vegetables, and occasionally a few coins. "Yes, there are big problems, big obstacles, and big challenges," Leyson says, "but I found here the real happiness of a fulfilled life."

Leyson became director of his father's Bible college, where he trained a group of faithful followers of Christ to make inroads into the Muslim community. In 2002, Leyson's efforts paid off when a breakthrough occurred. Less than a mile from a terrorist training camp, an underground church of former Muslims was established with the help of a young woman named Mary.

Mary's Ministry

Mary, who worked in ministry with the Leyson family while she was in high school, won a scholarship to Mindanao State University. The fact that the college was decidedly Muslim failed to hinder her resolve to spread the good news of Christ. Her vivacity and warm personality soon earned her the friendship of her classmates and professors.

Mary gradually began sharing her testimony, and one by one her friends gave their lives to Christ. She started a Bible study group—something the university forbade—for these new believers. Soon, every student in her dormitory was attending. She also secretly placed Christian books and Bibles in the school's library.

Some of Mary's Muslim classmates learned of her outreach and started sending her death threats. At one of her prayer meetings, several Muslim students threw stones at her and the other Christians. Another gathering was interrupted when Muslims shot guns into the air as a warning for her to discontinue. Mary went on with her ministry. "Prayer is our most powerful weapon," she said. "God hears our cries and delivers us from our enemies."

Mary decided to invite the same Muslim classmates who had threatened her to a meeting where Leyson had agreed to preach on the topic of love. This was a foreign concept to most Muslims, who are trained to know only duty, and Leyson knew he could be killed if his message was not well received. He made arrangements for someone to look after his body in that event, but the terror he felt as he crossed the threshold vanished when he walked to the front of the room. When he began his sermon, he was surprised at the strength and confidence in his voice.

Leyson looked out on a crowd of blank stares and crossed arms.

As he closed his message, five students in the back arose from their seats and began to walk forward. Leyson's heart began to pound. This could be his last day.

"We've come to accept Christ as our Savior," one of them said. The five kneeled down, and Leyson led them in prayer. These five students are now sharing Christ in their hometowns. Many who have witnessed the change in their behavior have also turned their lives over to Jesus.

The episode had a profound effect on Leyson's faith. "I realized that God will use us if we will stop making excuses," he says. "Serving God and using our life to God's glory is the greatest privilege of a believer."

Mary's campus ministry has continued to grow, and former Muslim students are now evangelizing, conducting prayer meetings, and discipling others.

> "I realized that God will use us if we will stop making excuses."

Making Disciples of All Men

Leyson continues to preach in Mindanao in addition to travelling to remote islands to evangelize unreached tribes. Most of the students at the Bible college are new converts of primitive tribes who wish to evangelize their own people. Leyson usually has to start from scratch with them, as the majority of these trainees come to the college completely illiterate.

"Most of them don't even know how old they are," says Leyson. "We have to guess their age and assign them a birthday."

Before the believers return to their own villages, they are given four years of basic education and biblical training. Toward the end of their education, the tribal missionaries are expected to begin evangelizing their own communities. The students alternate three weeks of ministry in their own village with one week of classroom training. For most, this means walking for several days through jungle terrain, air gun in hand to hunt for food along the way.

36

Baitan Ramos, who attends the Bible college, walks twenty-two miles to reach the church he planted in his village. Ramos was forced to drop out of school in the fourth grade because his parents could not afford to educate him. After he joined the New People's Army, he learned about Christ through one of Leyson's sermons, which was broadcast on the radio. He gave his life to Jesus and joined the Bible college.

These native missionaries-in-training come from extreme poverty. For most, the only clothing they own are T-shirts plastered with the faces of political leaders—items given to the general public for free during election time. Many have never worn a pair of shoes, so their toes are spread out in different directions. Leyson describes their feet as resembling a ginger root. For others, scraping together the means to feed their families is a tremendous chal-

> Many have never worn a pair of shoes, so their toes are spread out in different directions.

lenge. The large barrels of fish, brought to shore each morning by the fishermen of Mindanao, sell for five pesos (10 cents) a barrel—a price many cannot afford.

The financial support Christian Aid sends to Leyson's ministry is thinly spread to the gospel workers under his supervision. During his regular visits to each worker's respective mission field, he is usually able to leave them with a modest amount. Leyson maintains frequent communication with his gospel team and will drop everything if urgent help is needed. "They sacrifice, so I sacrifice," Leyson says.

Leyson's ministry continues to grow and reach people groups who have never heard the name of Christ. He currently ministers among twenty tribes.

—BT

Discover More!

Join us on Facebook to receive up-to-date stories and global mission news.

www.facebook.com/christianaid53

NEXT STORY ...

"For we walk by faith, not by sight."

—2 Corinthians 5:7

Bayani Leyson and Carlo Perez may live on opposite sides of the earth, but they have a lot in common. Both operate in the jungle, seeking out their nation's most feared inhabitants.

In the Philippines, Leyson reaches out to the cannibals. In Colombia, Perez shares Christ's love with the FARC, a formidable and barbarous insurgent group. Both of these men have been threatened, and both have nearly lost their lives. Yet it is a price they are willing to pay to follow God's leading.

Although these men's courage sometimes fails them, their faith drives them forward. The only way that either of them will stop is when God calls them home to their final destination. Until that day, they remain unstoppable.

COLOMBIA

Chapter 6

UNSTOPPABLE

Faith. Many times that is all Carlo Perez takes with him on his walks through the jungles of Colombia. Evil hides in the underbrush and around almost every corner in the path. But despite the threat, he marches forward, accompanied by four of his brothers in Christ.

The attack happened in a split second but seemed to unfold in slow motion. Perez watched as one of five robbers, who seemed to appear out of nowhere, unsheathed his machete and raised it high. The blade sliced through the air, and then through the skull of one of Perez's friends. The sound haunts him to this day—like an eggshell cracked on the side of a frying pan. The man shrieked as blood poured from his head. As Perez dove for cover, sliding into the mud under the foliage, he saw the gray tint of his friend's brain.

The sound haunts him to this day—like an eggshell cracked on the side of a frying pan.

The event was not atypical of the kind of danger Perez faces on a daily basis. He has been threatened, beaten, and robbed. He has watched helplessly as others in his ministry have been kidnapped or killed by military or guerrilla groups. When he was fourteen years old, terrorists killed his father. Perez, determined to avenge his father's death, joined the army at age twenty-one.

At age twenty-four, he married his wife, Rita. Only days later he was diagnosed with epilepsy and hospitalized for aggressive behavior. Perez's miraculous healing, after a pastor prayed over him, was the seed that bore his unshakeable faith and dynamic ministry.

"I was unstoppable," he says.

Making Disciples

Unable to resist the call of the jungle, Perez responds to it every single day. It's been that way since 1965. As the director of a large and growing ministry, he immerses himself in the training of native missionaries. Every six months, he holds training seminars for eager, future church-planters.

The number of Colombian missionaries continues to grow, and their testimonies are a tribute to God's redeeming power. Many of them are former thieves, alcoholics, sorcerers, fighters, or assassins.

Perez also trains young women to become Sunday school teachers. At the completion of their training, he sends them back to their home-towns with stacks of brightly colored shirts emblazoned with a gospel message—gifts for each child who attends their Sunday school classes. Grateful for their children's new clothing, poverty-stricken parents typically ask their children what they learned. The simple message of hope that follows often prompts them to learn more.

Hostile Territory

Perez's ministry operates on the eastern side of Colombia, which is dominated by the Revolutionary Armed Forces of Colombia (FARC), the oldest, largest and best-equipped insurgent force in the country. The FARC controls approximately 40 percent of the country and finances itself through kidnapping ransoms, extortion, and the drug trade.

The average FARC guerrilla earns almost double the wages of a civilian. The group is especially adept at recruiting youth, who are promised a better life than their impoverished parents can provide.

These youth are soon called upon to attack, rob, kidnap, and kill innocent people.

To avoid these guerrillas, many parents send their children to big cities, where there is less chance the group will recruit them. Perez's ministry has stra-

These youth are soon called upon to attack, rob, kidnap, and kill innocent people.

tegically planted churches in these cities. They work to provide food, clothing, and shelter to those who have come to escape the FARC.

The Colombian government, with its inadequate army, is powerless to protect its own people. It can only stand by as the FARC seizes the property of helpless inhabitants and forces them to evacuate their homes in search of other means of shelter. Perez's ministry workers have responded to this need by constructing a guesthouse for displaced persons in Bogotá, Colombia's capital city.

Members of the FARC are especially hostile toward evangelical Christians. Many times the guerrillas will attend a church meeting under cover to covertly monitor the service. "They are very sneaky," Perez says. "They appear legitimate because they know a few Scriptures and address others as 'brother' or 'sister'."

Changing Lives

Perez's ministry leaders are unable to take an offering during their meetings, as members of the FARC would confiscate the funds. For this reason, the financial assistance provided by Christian Aid has been an invaluable resource to the ministry. A Christian Aid field scout first discovered the group in 1987.

Perez takes advantage of the FARC's constant scrutiny of Christians, using it as an opportunity for evangelism. "It's the everyday living— being a good neighbor, inviting them in for dinner, a kind word—that will plant seeds in their hearts and eventually win them to Christ," Perez says.

Perez has already seen the effects of some of the seed his group has sown. Raul, a commander of a guerrilla group, murdered a man who attended a church planted by one of Perez's disciples. After learning about the tragedy, the pastor of the church visited Raul and told him about God's love and forgiveness. Raul was stunned by the pastor's gracious reaction to his ruthless deed and invited him to come back. The visits continued for several more months until Raul and his family accepted Christ as Savior.

Raul is just one of countless people won to Christ by the courageous love of Perez's missionaries, who are willing to risk their own lives to save the lives of others.

Perez is heading toward the finish line of his faithful race, but he is not doing so timidly. Even after surgery for six hernias, he heads for the jungle. You will find him on a motorcycle or in a canoe, making his way to a remote community in need of the gospel.

> Even after surgery for six hernias, he heads for the jungle.

Josué, his youngest son of five children, is preparing to oversee the ministry when the day comes that Perez can no longer work.

—BT

Discover More!

Did you know that the amount needed to support one American family overseas will provide an entire year of support for 10 to 40 native missionaries?

See the cost comparison chart online.

www.christianaid.org/ftt/6

NEXT STORY ...

"Lift up your heads, O ye gates; and be ye lift up, ye everlasting doors; and the King of glory shall come in. Who is this King of glory? The LORD strong and mighty, the LORD mighty in battle. Lift up your heads, O ye gates; even lift them up, ye everlasting doors; and the King of glory shall come in. Who is this King of glory? The LORD of hosts, He is the King of glory."
—Psalm 24:7–10

With prayer and persistence, the Lord's missionaries break barriers all over the earth. In Columbia, God lifts the gates of guerilla warfare as His faithful servants persevere through violent attacks to bring the gospel to remote areas.

In the former Soviet Union, the King of Glory lifted the iron curtain as godless walls of communism collapsed. But years of secret prayer and worship opened the way. In Ukraine, men like Slavik Radchuk, led by the Holy Spirit, believed for revival in their land. The King of Glory, strong and mighty, came with power.

Today, believers in this land do not waste a moment in calling young people to action. They know the time is short. Great freedom spread through the nations with the lifting of the curtain, but no one knows how long that freedom will remain. So these believers make the most of every opportunity. One day they will stand before the throne of God and know they did all they could to reach every village with the gospel.

RUSSIA

Chapter 7

CHURCH EXPLOSION IN THE FORMER SOVIET UNION

Slavik Radchuk stirred from his sleep as footsteps echoed in the hall. The door creaked.

"Slavik, wake up," his father whispered.

The pre-dawn dimness enfolded him like a dream. He would have stayed beneath his covers, but the Lord called. As he journeyed with his dad to the meeting place, the Word rose in his heart. Every moment counted.

At fourteen, Slavik was the oldest of eight children. During the summer months, he held the gospel in his heart and preached at the secret gathering in the forest. During the winter, the underground believers worshiped in a small apartment.

Communist authorities could easily squelch these assemblies in Ukraine, so the anticipation mounted as the believers greeted one another at 6 A.M. in the open air. They prayed with power. Slavik preached with faith. One day, revival would come. He would carry the Word to his people.

> One day, revival would come. He would carry the Word to his people.

Paying the Price

In his youth, Slavik spent time with godly, elderly men of faith. He was curious as to how he could build the Kingdom of God. At sixteen, he asked one man to pray for him.

"Are you ready?" the wise man said.

"Yes," Slavik answered. He felt the fire of God in his heart.

Later, he heard the still, quiet voice of the Holy Spirit ask him the same question. "Are you ready to pay the price?" the voice said.

Tears flowed like rain down Slavik's cheeks. "Yes," he answered. "I am ready to pay the price."

The gospel must go forth. In the years to come, one believer after another would end up in prison, but he would continue to preach the gospel. For as Jesus says, "Go into all the world and preach the gospel to every creature" (Mark 16:15, NKJV).

Revival Prayer

In Ukraine, the communists forbade families to teach their children about Christ. Of the 800 children in his school, only Slavik served the Lord.

During the Soviet days, believers savored secret prayer meetings, where approximately 200 would gather and pray all night. In 1980, they learned from visiting Swedish Christians that there were 170 people groups, or nations, in the former Soviet Union. One night, they wrote each nation's name on slips of paper and placed them face down on a table. Each in attendance came forward to take a piece of paper and pray for a nation.

"God, please send revival," they prayed.

Slavik felt the fullness of God in his heart. "Revival is coming," he said. "The harvest is coming."

With hundreds of pastors in jail, his friends struggled to believe.

Missions Begin

In 1984, Sergei Sharapa and Slavik Radchuk traveled as spies—like Joshua and Caleb—across the former Soviet Union to see where the gospel could be preached. At that time they could fly from Moscow to

Vladivostok for only $15. They found people who worshipped the sun, the moon, and the rocks, but who had never heard about the Lord Jesus Christ.

The next year, Slavik and two brothers joined a team of missionaries and went to Tuva, located in southern Siberia. There they preached the gospel and saw hundreds of people come to Christ. The rumblings of revival stirred in every meeting. But when the KGB heard, they told the citizens via television to avoid the gospel preachers. They ordered Slavik's group to leave.

Slavik and his team returned home and continued to pray. In 1986, they split into five smaller groups, and each recruited more volunteers. They covered another five areas: Abakan, Irkutsk, Komsomolsk, Angarsk, and Kyzyl.

Mikhail Gorbachev became party head in 1985. He introduced *glasnost,* a policy that called for increased government openness in the Soviet Union, and *perestroika,* which called for a restructuring of the communist party. By 1988, Slavik and his group were enjoying complete freedom. They celebrated 1,000 years of Christianity in Russia, dating from the baptism of Prince Vladimir of Kiev in AD 988.

Slavik knew the time had come for revival. He approached the mayor of Rivne and asked to conduct a crusade. "I want to rent an outdoor place big enough to accommodate 10,000 people," he said.

"Are you crazy?" the mayor asked.

Slavik showed him a newspaper announcing Gorbachev's new policies. The mayor was astounded, but seeing it in the newspaper caused him to believe.

First Big Crusade

About 20,000 people turned out for the first big crusade in Ukraine. Slavik went on to hold crusades all over Ukraine and the former Soviet Union. He saw tens of thousands come to Christ.

Ukraine became the hub for the gospel. From there, Slavik's group sent missionaries all over Russia, including Siberia. Assisted by Christian Aid, Good Samaritan Mission sent 125 missionaries to this region. Voice of Hope, also helped by Christian Aid, sent out 110. Others went as well.

The land once closed to Christianity has now birthed churches all across the former Soviet Empire. In Tashkent, Uzbekistan, for instance, one church now has 10,000 adult members and 4,000 children. The fellowship also has started 150 new churches in Karakalpakstan, Turkmenistan, Kyrgyzstan, and Tajikistan.

> The land once closed to Christianity has now birthed churches all across the former Soviet Empire.

Church Explosion

In 1990, Uzbekistan had only twenty-one evangelical churches. That number reached 820 just thirteen years later. Most are house churches filled with young people.

In neighboring Kyrgyzstan, 728 evangelical churches have surfaced. Nearly half the believers come from Muslim backgrounds. Today the people realize freedom of religion, yet persecution has increased.

Tajikistan hosts 110 evangelical churches.

In Russia, just 480 evangelical churches existed in 1990. Today, more than 28,000 churches fill that nation.

In Belarus, 2,100 churches worship the Lord. Soviet-style laws keep congregations of less than 100 members from registering to meet, yet the churches there have grown faster than in Ukraine. One church alone has 1,000 members.

Multiplication in Ukraine

Christian Aid helped purchase 125 former government-owned buildings for new churches. Faith Bible School, operated by Good Samaritan Mission, has trained and sent out 115 workers. These workers go as missionaries, plant churches, and become pastors for the communities.

Many of these churches start daughter churches. One new church in Ukraine has already planted fifteen other churches. In 1990 there were 550 evangelical churches in Ukraine. Fifteen years later, there were 9,500.

Many Tatars who were sent to Siberia by Stalin have returned to their homes in Crimea and are open to the gospel. Voice of Hope missionaries have started churches among them.

Emmanuel Mission planted 140 churches and opened three orphanages. Its main church has 1,600 members.

Christian Aid sent funds to build Salvation Church near Kiev. The congregation constructed a building that will seat 2,000 people. More than 2,500 members attend that church. Children from an organization known as Father's House go there.

Father's House

The church explosion in the former Soviet Union inspired a transformation in children's homes.

In 1997, volunteer missionary workers opened an emergency shelter in a rented apartment for twenty to thirty boys. They called this shelter "Father's House."

As the missionaries went out to search the night streets and hand out nutritious food to abandoned children, they came upon an underground world. Children lived in basement hovels, made their own laws, and even had a "mafia." If they died, no one ever found them.

At the shelter, these children received hot meals, a bath, and clean clothes. They also heard the gospel. Many eventually gave their lives to Christ.

Father's House now cares for 1,200 boys and girls. Thanks to the generosity of Christian Aid donors, more than twenty Father's House children's centers are currently operating in Ukraine—and lives are being saved.

This is revolutionary, because the state used to control all orphanages.

Government statistics report that Kiev used to have 60 percent Orthodox believers and barely two percent evangelical believers. Now the numbers show that possibly 40 percent of believers are Orthodox and 40 percent are evangelical. Some churches have 20,000 members.

Approximately 95 percent of the new believers are young people.

> Approximately 95 percent of the new believers are young people.

Youth Movement

Even with the growth of Christianity and the birth of new churches during the last twenty-five years, some 120,000 villages and cities in the former Soviet Union have still never heard the gospel. Many have no church or witness among them. In Ukraine, the number of unreached villages is 25,000.

To meet this need, leaders began inviting young people to give one year of their lives to Jesus as missionaries. Working together in teams, they move from south to north to place four New Testaments in every village. When they have an opportunity, they share the gospel with the people. In this way, what began as a church explosion has become a youth movement all across Ukraine and the former Soviet Union.

"Maybe in a few years I can report that we delivered New Testaments and were able to preach the gospel in all Russia and all the former Soviet Union—in every village, in every city," Slavik says. "When we come before God's holy throne, we can say we did everything to witness to our people. All nations must come before His holy throne."

For seventy years, Bibles were forbidden in the former Soviet Union. Ladies secretly copied the Scriptures by hand, working ten years to produce a single Bible. An underground church of 300 members huddled around five Bibles. Those who were caught with a page of Scripture in their homes were arrested and imprisoned for three to five years.

"When we come before God's holy throne, we can say we did everything to witness to our people. All nations must come before His holy throne."

Today, however, Bibles are being printed in the former USSR. People who have known only communism now behold the Word of God.

An older lady who knew communism her whole life had never heard the gospel. When young indigenous missionaries visited her village and stopped to share with her, she listened and believed. They handed her a copy of the New Testament, and she wept because the knowledge of the glory of the Lord had come to her. Once blind, she now could see. Once hidden, the gospel now had reached her heart.

The youth continue to make their way across that land to prayerfully plant a witness for Christ—through the Scriptures—in every village and city. They pay the price of taking the gospel, as they sleep where temperatures reach 70 degrees below zero.

A $5 gift will put four New Testaments in one village.

From a church explosion to a youth movement, the Lord continues to move in power in Ukraine and the former Soviet Union. And Slavik proclaims the Word from his heart.

—JH

Discover More!

Want your church to be more involved in indigenous missions? Find resources online to help influence and impact your pastor and congregation.

www.christianaid.org/ftt/7

NEXT STORY ...

"The cowering prisoners will soon be set free; they will not die in their dungeon, nor will they lack bread."

—Isaiah 51:14, NIV

The believers in the former Soviet Union were oppressed under communist rule, yet underground churches prayed in faith. The Lord's faithful servants suffered captivity, but victory came. The iron curtain collapsed, and the worshipers of Jesus arose to take their place—in the open.

During the Cultural Revolution in China, thousands endured torturous prison labor camps for their faith. Today, Chinese believers exhibit an unsurpassed hunger for the truth of God's Word. An estimated 100 million Chinese Christians boldly attend churches that are not registered with the communist government.

Christian Aid's China Division strengthens churches and Bible schools across the provinces. Not all remain underground.

As workers in the China Division travelled to search out worthy ministries, they discovered a hidden treasure—a registered school at the heart of a registered church, each radiating Christ with the devotion of the most underground worshipers.

Jesus said, "A city that is set on a hill cannot be hidden" (Matthew 5:14, NKJV). So shines Handan Christian Bible School in Handan Province. Prayer unlocks the city gates, and Priscilla Liu, the leader of this school, holds the key.

CHINA

Chapter 8

DEEP DEVOTION IN CHINA

Priscilla Liu leads on her knees. If she calls others to pray for China, she first prepares the way.

When the buzzer sounds at 5 A.M., the students at Handan Christian Bible School rise and make their way to the prayer room, where Priscilla is already kneeling. Her knees press into the cold, hard floor. Students file in and bow beside her. They lean forward against benches or fold up like grasshoppers, face down.

They cry out to the Lord.

Every morning, seven days a week, the 122 young men and women rise at the sound of the alarm and gather in one of the prayer rooms in the five-story building. Every evening, they meet again to close the day.

On their knees. In surrender. Yet in the power of the Lord.

Prayer forges the path. From prayer flows every good work.

While Handan Christian Bible School is government-registered, Priscilla worships the Lord Jesus with steadfast devotion. She follows all regulations, but she never relents in weeping prayers and teaching the cross. There is power in the blood of Christ Jesus.

The foundations run deep here.

This Bible school began in the heart of its leader.

Priscilla Liu's Dedication

Born in 1963, Priscilla met Dorothy Sun, director of Christian Aid's China Division, in 1981 after Dorothy was released from prison. Dorothy had served twenty years in prison work camps for confessing Jesus as Lord. After her case was reversed and she was released from jail, she spent time visiting her Christian friends. One was Teacher "Auntie" Zhang, an old classmate of her mother's, who had become Priscilla's spiritual leader and Bible teacher.

> Dorothy had served twenty years in prison work camps for confessing Jesus as Lord.

Priscilla had just graduated from Jin Ling Theological Seminary in Beijing. This fifty-year-old school had been reinstated after the Cultural Revolution as a "democratic window display" to show the world that China had religious freedom, even though the Three-Self-Patriotic Movement Committee (TSPM) still held control.

Priscilla came from a devout Christian family in Inner Mongolia. Gifted in skill and pure in heart, she clung to the Lord Jesus and longed for more of God. Not satisfied with her seminary studies, she spent years learning from Teacher Zhang. She dedicated her life to the Lord for the gospel's sake and counted the cost of remaining single.

In 1991, Dorothy and her husband, Freddie Sun, began to establish and support underground Bible study fellowships at Freddie's aunt's place. Aunt Grace Wang was Teacher Zhang's neighbor. House churches and Bible studies thrived in both homes.

Priscilla was eager to start a Bible school. The fellowship prayed, and step-by-step the Lord led them to rent a building that was once the Empress Dowager's Summer House. The building drooped and creaked, but it would work.

The Beginnings of the School

Handan Christian Bible School emerged with three teachers, forty-eight students, and a cook. The students came by recommendations from house-church leaders. They arrived empty-handed, with barely more than the shirts on their backs, so Priscilla waived their tuition, room, and board fees. House churches donated rice and vegetables for simple meals. The students studied the New and Old Testaments and the Major and Minor Prophets.

The dilapidated facility made for cheap rent. Because the house had no kitchen, the students ate outside. Eventually, they collected bricks and wood to build an indoor kitchen. Cracks splintered down the classroom walls. The windows jammed, and the roof leaked. The students lived at the school but had no beds, so they made soil beds by building brick platforms and filling them with dirt.

The Lord loved the students, and they loved the Lord. They willingly and joyfully accepted all He provided. Through Christian Aid, Freddie and Dorothy visited them yearly, supporting them financially and spiritually through preaching, teaching, and counseling. The couple stayed and ate with the students.

In 1993, Priscilla and her team acquired a piece of land from South Church, a government-registered body of 2,000 believers in Handan City. They started a formal Bible school, building one floor after another, year after year. Through Christian Aid, many faithful donors continually supported the school.

Today, the school of 122 students comprises two main buildings. The five-story building includes a full basement, classrooms, library, dorms, and several prayer rooms. Another building two stories high holds a worship room and piano practice studios on the upper floor, while the dining room and kitchen occupy the first floor. Once each week a big pot of hard-boiled eggs covers the stove—a treat to accompany a steady diet of rice and vegetables.

Priscilla equips the students through solid biblical studies and teaching on the way of the cross. She leads by example, and the students, who long to know the Lord, follow her. The school's motto is "BE a living stone," and these "living stones" live a life of prayer. From prayer flow all ministries.

Impact on the Churches

The devotion of the students in the Bible school impacts church growth across Handan City. In a city of stifling smog, these young men and women bring a fresh breath of life as they serve churches, their community, and each other in the name of Jesus. They live and eat simply as they work hard for a one- to two-year term, training to win their country to Christ as missionaries, teachers, preachers, and worship leaders.

> In a city of stifling smog, these young men and women bring a fresh breath of life.

This school makes a difference.

Because the school is registered and ministers alongside South Church, the students have the freedom to evangelize and openly serve in more than forty meeting locations in the community. Underground schools don't have the same freedom. The students lead Bible studies, prayer meetings, men's and women's fellowship groups, and church services. Their reputation of devotion and excellence places them in high demand in the city.

In addition, because the students come from diverse tribes, villages, and churches, their impact reaches beyond the community to neighboring provinces. Trained in the Bible, prayer, and good works, they return after their studies are complete to reach their own communities for Christ.

Locally, the fruit tells the story of this school's success. The students and teachers lead lives of discipline and devotion, growing deep in their faith while reaching out to others. Prepared to suffer for Christ, they embrace hardship. Through prayer and practical training in serving, studying, cleaning, fitness, and farming, they make themselves ready for anything they must face. Their character is pure and tested.

Priscilla and her team teach "Christ and Him crucified," just as the underground Bible schools do, though the government challenges this idea. Her team faces persecution because of the message of the cross, but somehow they have been given favor to remain as they follow regulations.

They stay on their knees, and the presence of the Lord rests on them.

Hidden Behind the Churches

Beyond the Bible school, Priscilla serves as an elder in the government-registered South Church in Handan. Handan's three large registered churches are located to the south, west, and north parts of the city, with the school on the east side.

Although the school is registered, it has a "hidden" quality, much as an old oak tree has roots that stretch deeply into the earth to drink from secret streams. South Church works as a buffer for the school. The students attend the church and serve its fellowship as they grow through their school studies during the week.

Although the school is registered, it has a "hidden" quality, much as an old oak tree has roots that stretch deeply into the earth to drink from secret streams.

David Liu leads the fellowship group at South Church and teaches at the school. A former student from Handan Bible School, Priscilla invited him to serve as a teacher after his graduation. David preaches at the church two to three times per month on Sundays and also leads worship. In addition, he leads a group of 200 young men and women believers in weekly Bible study, prayer meetings, leadership training, and evangelism outings.

David, who has a wife and a two-year-old child, makes a meager salary of just $200 per month. Although this is a sacrifice, it is one that he willingly accepts. God faithfully calls His leaders and draws His students.

Two Testimonies

On Carol Yuan-Yuan Chai's first day at Handan, she saw big words on the blackboard that said, "Who led you here? What are you doing here?" She was sure the Lord had led her there, and she knew that she would focus her mind, heart, and spirit on her studies and be equipped by the Bible teachers. She shares her experience as a student:

A couple of days later, I was touched by the Lord, and I touched His hands. This is a school of prayer. I began to see my own sins and ugliness—that I needed my Lord's mercy and help.

The teachings here are special. The teachers faithfully teach the way of the cross and are willing to pay the price to walk that path joyfully. Although their salaries are meager and their meals are simple, they are drawn by the love of the Lord. Others who do not hold to the Truth slander them, but they endure patiently.

I know that the cross is not only a slogan I proclaim but also a daily step-by-step walk as I carry my own cross to follow Jesus. I thank the Lord for allowing me to meet Aunt Dorothy Sun of Christian Aid. She said, "The Lord needs young people to stand up for Jesus bravely and take the baton from the older generation."

I was so touched by that calling, but I have nothing to give to the Lord except my heart. I want to belong to Him totally. The older generation has touched our lives by their example and testimonies. I want to walk the same path.

May the Lord complete Himself in my life. My hope for this school is that more teachers will come and that one day soon it will become a seminary.

Xue-Tao Lu, another student at Handan, also believes that the Lord clearly led him to the school. He shares his thoughts:

I see daily the wonderful spirit in this school. I see a team of servants of God who joyfully and willingly carry their crosses to serve the Lord and the brothers and sisters.

The teacher who touched my life the most is Priscilla. She shows her great love and faithfulness to the Lord each day through her devoted life. In this wicked world I rarely see Christian servants who are willing to pay the price to walk daily, deny themselves, and carry their cross to follow Jesus.

It is also rare to see servants who have such passion to protect biblical truths or who live a life of wanting nothing for themselves and everything for God. This is the spirit of Handan Christian Bible School.

Our school has already existed for twenty years. It has gone from a poor collapsed building to a five-story building; from forty students to 122. We even have a little library now and about 8,000 good spiritual books.

The school focuses not only on equipping its students with Bible knowledge but also on building up their spiritual lives. The teachers never rely on the power of any person or governments. They only rely on faith in Christ, who is the author and finisher of our faith.

I can see the Lord with us every day. I praise the Lord for my student life in this school. We have 5 A.M. devotions, and then we head to classes. Every Saturday afternoon we go out to evangelize the community. On Sundays we serve the Lord at various churches.

I especially enjoy our school fellowship life. We take turns cleaning up all the facilities and dorms and work on our little farm. We have successfully planted fruit trees and vegetables, and together we enjoy the harvest. We also exercise by playing ping-pong, volleyball, badminton, and by going jogging.

I pray that my school will grow to become a formal theological seminary. All by God's grace.

The government officers of the Three-Self-Patriotic Movement Committee persecute the leaders. They criticize our school for being too strict with Christ-centered ways. But I am proud of my school for exactly that.

I want to be a teacher just like Priscilla. I want to serve the Lord with a pure heart, despising glory from men.

Glory to God

The school begins recruiting new students each year in May. More than 200 apply annually, but only 100 make it through the meticulous selection process to win an in-person interview. The prospects pay their own fares to visit for the interview.

Once selected, the students move in, find their bunks, and prepare their hearts for that 5 A.M. buzzer awakening, when prayer will draw them into a life of love and devotion. With joy they walk in the footsteps of their teachers in a world once tightly shut to the gospel. They freely worship, yet they understand the government's gaze.

But these students also understand that the doors are open. They boldly witness their faith. The gospel goes out in Handan, and it will reach across China.

Through prayer and supplication, fasting and discipleship, preaching and evangelism, and study and dedication, these young Chinese students are taking the baton and running the Lord's race for their generation— and for His glory.

—JH

Discover More!

Donate today to help support Christian Aid in their strategic support of indigenous missions.

www.christianaid.org/ftt/8

NEXT STORY ...

"But thou, Bethlehem Ephratah, though thou be little among the thousands of Judah, yet out of thee shall he come forth unto me that is to be ruler in Israel; whose goings forth have been from of old, from everlasting."
—Micah 5:2

Roving tigers, barbaric drug lords, and Islamic terrorists are not the only challenges missionaries encounter as they carry the good news to the uttermost corners of the earth. Sometimes the fiercest battle rages within their own souls. Soldiers of the cross aren't superheroes; they are humble servants used mightily by God when they surrender their dreams, talents, and even their disappointments to Him.

At times the forces of evil may seem overpowering, but God's light radiates hope in the midst of the darkness. Like the star pointing the wise men to the Savior's birthplace 2,000 years ago, Bethlehem Bible College shines as one of those guiding lights in the center of a sacred but deeply divided land. As the only Christian seminary in Palestine, the school serves a crucial role in training Arab believers to lead the church and be a witness for peace through Jesus Christ among their Muslim and Jewish neighbors.

Before Bethlehem Bible College could become a reality, however, its founder had to confront his own heart of darkness. Bishara Awad survived the Arab-Israeli war in 1948, but the wounds of war remained raw decades later. Bishara was a Christian, he loved God, and he had committed his life to serving in the ministry. He thought he was doing all the right things, but try as he might, his anger still burned against those responsible for his family's heartache. Would he ever be able to truly forgive and experience peace? Bishara realized his ministry would not prosper until he asked God for healing.

ISRAEL

Chapter 9

A BEACON OF LIGHT
IN BETHLEHEM

Nine-year-old Bishara lived with his family in the quiet Jerusalem neighborhood of Musrara, outside the walls of the Old City. The community, lined with rows of lovely stone houses, had been founded by Arab Christians in the late 1800s. They took pride in their heritage, and their homeland they called *Filastin,* the Arabic word for Palestine.

For Elias and Huda Awad, raising their seven children to love and follow Jesus Christ was of paramount importance. They attended the Greek Orthodox church together and sometimes went to the Church of God, where Bishara's uncle served as pastor. While the rest of the world seemed to be caught up in a cataclysmic war, the Awads enjoyed a peaceful co-existence with their Jewish and Muslim neighbors. But their idyllic life would soon change forever.

On May 14, 1948, Israel officially became an independent nation following the termination of the British Mandate. War erupted almost immediately between Jewish Zionists and the Jordanian army that stormed in to protect Palestine's Arab population. The city of Musrara, poised in a strategic location, lay directly in the crossfire. Heavy fighting kept residents in Bishara's neighborhood indoors. Many families had already evacuated the city, but with the wellbeing of seven children to consider, Elias and Huda had nowhere to go. They were among several Christian families who were trapped in the war zone.

A walk to the store to buy groceries was too dangerous. Elias could not travel to his job as a laundry services manager at the hospital in West Jerusalem. Bishara and his siblings—Nicola, the oldest at eleven; Elizabeth; Ellen; Mubarak; Alex; and six-month-old Diana—longed to go outside and play. At Huda's insistence, they couldn't even peer out the windows. Their small but comfortable home began to feel like a prison for them, their parents, and their grandmother Nyfeh.

Tragedy and Flight

One week after the start of the conflict, the Awads enjoyed a day of relative quiet. Sounds of machine guns and explosions had ceased. Elias stepped out of the building to get some fresh air.

Suddenly, Bishara heard screams and shouts for help coming from the street. He ran to the window and realized the anguished voice was his mother's.

Bishara stared in horror. Lying in the street was the still figure of his father. Huda leaned over him, her hand clutching his head.

Nicola was the first to reach their parents, with Bishara close behind. Neighbors left the safety of their houses to help and carried the wounded man into the house. They lifted him onto a table, where Huda attempted to resuscitate her husband. But it was too late. The bullet that struck Elias Awad in the head had killed him instantly.

With no pastor or priest available, the family dug a shallow grave the next day in a patch of earth behind their house. Huda read from her Bible, and the children joined in saying the Lord's Prayer before laying their beloved father to rest.

Although they could never say for certain who killed Elias, the type of bullet and the direction from which it was fired indicated that it came from an Israeli paramilitary sniper stationed in the vicinity of Notre Dame Cathedral. Young Bishara lost more than his father during that devastating week. The nightmare of war had only just begun to permeate his life and emotions.

A month later, Huda was preparing the children for bed when the sound of fists pounding at the front door disrupted their solemn evening. The unexpected visit came from soldiers, spreading the word among Musrara's remaining residents to evacuate immediately. The Israeli army was bearing down on the neighborhood and would arrive within minutes.

The soldiers advised Huda to not even run upstairs and grab her purse. Dressed in their sleepwear, the children only had time to wrap themselves in blankets. Bishara's sister, Ellen, just five years old, didn't want to leave her prettiest dresses behind. With no time to change clothes, she hastily put a handful of them on—wearing several layers of dresses over the top of her nightgown.

The Awads joined others in a mad flight to the Old City in Jerusalem. It was a short journey, and they assumed that after the conflict was over, they would simply return to their homes in Musrara. None of them could have envisioned that they would never live in their hometown again—the place where they had buried Bishara's father.

The family's sufferings mirrored that of some 750,000 Palestinians— Christian and Muslim alike—who became refugees in the ensuing months as they fled hundreds of towns and villages where their families had lived for generations.

Hope School

As Bishara walked down the hallway toward his office, he took note of the defeated demeanor of several students. They greeted him cordially enough, out of respect perhaps for his position at the school, but their slumped shoulders and downcast eyes belied deep emotional wounds that he wished he could erase.

Bishara was discouraged as well. Now in his mid-thirties, he had found God's calling for him in the educational field. He loved being the principal of Hope Secondary School on the outskirts of Bethlehem, where he planted seeds of faith in the hearts of the 100 boys placed under his care. However, something was wrong.

Bishara shook his head in frustration. He was pouring so much of himself into the lives of these youth. They were hearing the gospel message, reading God's Word, and praying and worshipping together, but he saw no fruit. Not one of the students had received Christ as their Savior in months.

He thought about their struggles. Some had lost one or both parents in the never-ending conflict between the Palestinians and Israelis. Others had lost their homes. They suffered daily oppression and intimidation. As students, they experienced the humiliation of bullying soldiers who searched their backpacks, tossed their books into the dirt, and commanded them to pick them up. Feeling defenseless, the youth would sometimes throw rocks at the soldiers.

The pain and resentment Bishara saw on the faces of these Palestinian boys reflected his own childhood angst. After his family became refugees, they had the option to move into overcrowded camps run by the Red Cross. But Huda chose instead to place her children in boarding schools and orphanages that took in youngsters on a charity basis. Meanwhile, she rented a small apartment, found a job paying $25 a month at a hospital, and enrolled in school to become a registered nurse so she could eventually make a better life for herself and her children.

Bishara and two of his brothers lived in a boys' home in Jerusalem. They studied at St. George's School, a prestigious academic institution run by the Church of England, which awarded scholarships to students who lost one or both parents during the 1948 war. The brothers were blessed to receive a first-class education that Huda could never have afforded for them.

A Transforming Work

Despite these perks, life in the boarding school was lonesome, as the boys didn't see their mother or other siblings for weeks or even months at a time. They looked forward to the holidays, when they would be reunited as a family in their mother's cramped apartment. But the absence of their father continued to grieve their hearts.

Bishara went on to attend Dakota Wesleyan University in the United States on a full scholarship. He graduated in 1964 with a bachelor's degree in mathematics and a minor in chemistry. He was pursuing a master's degree in education at a college in Missouri when war broke out yet again in Palestine.

As a result of the Six Day War of 1967, Israel gained control of additional territory that included East Jerusalem and the West Bank. The government instituted a policy whereby Palestinians who were living abroad could not return to their homeland. The only way Bishara could now return to Palestine was to become a United States citizen, so that's what he did. In the interim, he taught high school in Kansas City for several years and, through the auspices of a Mennonite organization, returned to Palestine in 1972 to be the principal of Hope School.

Bishara's mother had often advised her children, "Never revenge the death of your father. Always show the love of Christ to the Jews, to Muslims, to everyone." These words pierced his heart.

Hadn't he forgiven those who had stolen so much from him? Was he still harboring deep bitterness in his heart? Bishara tasted the acrid rage that rose inside of him just thinking about the injustice he had endured.

In his book *Light Force,* Brother Andrew of Open Doors Ministries recounts the transforming work God performed in Bishara's heart that spring night in 1974:

> Bishara blamed the Israelis for the death of his father and the loss of his home in 1948. He blamed them for the twelve years he'd lived in an orphanage, separated from his mother. He blamed them for the years of exile in the United States. For so long the hatred had festered, mostly below his consciousness. Now he recognized that same hatred in the boys under his care. It was destroying them, and he was powerless to help them unless he, their principal, conquered his own anger and bitterness.
>
> Tears welled up in his eyes. How could he, a man who had given his life to Jesus Christ a dozen years before, who was committed to be an instrument of God in the Holy Land, help these angry young boys? There was only one answer. His voice broke the silence of the night: "Lord, I beg You. Forgive me for hating the Jews and for allowing that hatred to control my life."
>
> With every ounce of his being, Bishara meant that prayer…. He sensed God's presence enveloping him, and the frustration, hopelessness, and hatred were washed away, replaced with love.[1]

A New Mission

Now that Bishara's heart had been softened, he was ready for the greater purpose God had awaiting him. He began to go about his daily work

---

[1]Brother Andrew and Al Janssen, *Light Force: A Stirring Account of the Church Caught in the Middle East Crossfire* (Grand Rapids, MI: Revell, 2004), pp. 106–107.

at Hope School with a more compassionate spirit. The boys noticed. The Holy Spirit was working in a mighty way, and the students began committing their hearts to Christ and pursuing Christian ministry after they graduated.

For years the large exodus of Christians out of Palestine, the Land of the Bible, had dismayed Bishara. Before 1948, approximately 8 percent of the population was Christian. Since that time, the number had dropped to a mere one and a half percent. Some had left because their homes had been destroyed in the 1948 and 1967 wars, while others had gone because of the area's 30 percent unemployment rate or frustration over Israeli checkpoints and restricted travel. Most disappointing was to see promising graduates of Hope School leave the country in order to receive seminary training. Few of them ever returned to serve churches in Palestine.

"The Lord gave me a vision that what we need here in Bethlehem is a Bible college," says Bishara. "I shared this vision with pastors and church leaders, and they all agreed. One pastor gave me a check and said, 'Bishara, you can do it.' I looked at the check. It was for $20."

Other organizations supplied additional seed funds. In 1979, Bethlehem Bible College began its inaugural semester with nine students. Missionaries taught evening courses held at Hope School, where Bishara still served as principal.

God continued to deliver miracles. Two years later, Bishara realized the school needed its own facility, so he began to pray they could purchase three vacant buildings that were formerly occupied by the Helen Keller Home for the Blind in Bethlehem. The owner agreed to give the Bible college rent-free use of the site for five years. After that time, they would have to come up with the money to purchase the buildings. Bishara was granted a one-year extension, and through God's provision, the college raised the funds to buy the $1.8 million property and transform it into a beautiful campus.

Today, Bethlehem Bible College is an interdenominational accredited four-year institution that trains Palestinian men and women to become Christian leaders in ministry, mass media, tourism, and education. Each year, the school enrolls about 150 to 200 students at the main campus and its satellite locations in Galilee and Gaza.

Advanced degrees are also offered. The master's program in Christian Leadership continues to grow in popularity, and there are future plans to add a similar specialization in Peace Studies. Once it is implemented, the program will be the only one of its kind taught in the Middle East.

Bishara, whose name means "good news" in Arabic, has seen God bless the ministry of Bethlehem Bible College beyond measure. The school has filled a pivotal role as it endeavors to keep a Christian presence in Palestine and build up churches in the region.

"For us it would have been a shame if Bethlehem, where Jesus was born, was emptied of the Christian witness and light for the Lord," Bishara muses. "The Bible college is one instrument by which we keep Christians here. We train them here, and once they graduate they stay in the land. We are very grateful for that."

The Shepherd's Society

Over the past fifteen years, Christian Aid has helped support The Shepherd's Society, the humanitarian arm of the ministry. Through outreach to the community, Bible students share the love of Jesus with needy Palestinian families by giving out food baskets, ministering to widows, and doing vocational training.

The ministry provides assistance to Christians and Muslims, and the annual Christmas celebration draws some 1,000 people for a meal and an evangelistic service. Dozens come forward to receive Christ as their personal Savior. Students follow up with new believers and work closely with local churches to ensure these individuals are plugged into a fellowship where they can grow in their walk with the Lord.

In September 2012, Bishara stepped down from his leadership role after thirty-three years of shepherding the flock at Bethlehem Bible College. He currently serves as president emeritus. Succeeding him as president is Jack Sara, the former pastor of an evangelical church in Jerusalem and a graduate of Bethlehem Bible College.

Bishara believes there is hope for the inhabitants of Palestine— whether Christian, Muslim, or Jew. That hope is rooted in the Prince of Peace, whose humble birth in Bethlehem brought forth the gift of salvation to all mankind.

"What do we do with these challenges?" Bishara says. "As Christians, we seek the Lord, we pray for peace, and we pray that one day the Israelis and Palestinians will come together and work out a peace agreement so that both groups can live in that part of the world. The big task is to keep Christians here, to be a light for the Lord Jesus in the Holy Land."

—VD

Discover More!

Join us in prayer and action by donating to specific Prayerline needs.

www.christianaid.org/ftt/9

EUROPE

Chapter 10

RED BALL EXPRESS
By Bob Finley

In June 1944, Allied forces invaded Normandy and moved rapidly eastward into France to face the German army. By late July, the German front cracked and the Allied troops began a frantic chase after the rapidly retreating German soldiers.

As General Patton's army swept through France, charging ahead toward victory, it burned up nearly 400,000 gallons of gasoline per day. A few weeks later, the Allies' reserves were completely exhausted. The army needed a steady supply of fuel if they were to keep moving.

Meanwhile, the Germans awaited the inevitable moment when the Allied troops would run out of food, water, ammunition, and fuel for their tanks and military vehicles. In all other wars, when forces had advanced too far too soon, they had run out of resources. The defenders would then counterattack and defeat them.

But this time the outcome was different.

Enter the Red Ball Express

Nearly 95 percent of the Allies' resources sat at base depots along the coast of Normandy, where American ships had delivered them. The supplies would have remained completely useless to frontline soldiers, who had no way to access them, if not for a massive supply line of approximately 6,000 trucks. This was the key to delivering the crucial resources to the frontlines.

The army collected trucks from all units that could spare them. They enlisted soldiers whose duties were not critical to the immediate war effort to serve as drivers. The army called the operation the Red Ball Express, after the railroad phrase to "red ball" it, or ship it express.

The army blocked off a highway for the use of the express drivers and covered it in signs plastered with a big red ball that guided the drivers forward. Convoys of five trucks each, overloaded with supplies, drove around the clock. The drivers often ignored the speed limits and raced ahead toward the fast-moving front. Rest stops were set up along the route so the drivers could stop for a hot meal.

With their needs supplied in this manner, the Allied troops continued their advance, and the Germans were unable to stop them. The Red Ball Express proved to be the most important factor in the rapid defeat of the German army. For three months it transported resources over distances up to 400 miles. In all, it delivered more than 500,000 tons of supplies to the front lines.

> The Red Ball Express proved to be the most important factor in the rapid defeat of the German army.

A Different Kind of Supply Line

Just as the Red Ball Express helped the Allied forces win battles during World War II, Christian Aid is now helping soldiers in God's Kingdom win more crucial battles. The frontline troops today are native missionaries in almost every country who serve Christ with indigenous mission boards. Most of these missionaries are in lands of poverty and persecution, where local support is not available. The supply lines are individual Christians and Bible-believing churches in industrialized countries.

Many of the unreached people groups these native missionaries target live in bondage to false religions. Bound by the fear of displeasing fictitious deities, they offer precious sacrifices of food to pagan gods— food that could be used to feed their hungry families. When a native missionary enters their village, many are drawn to the irresistible joy and peace that radiates from the true freedom found only in Christ. Chains are broken and souls rejoice when the good news penetrates the hearts of those who were trapped in the enemy's camp. A battle is won for the Kingdom of God.

But this battle for souls is no easy task. There is always a counterattack. These new believers almost always experience hardship. Depending on the country, the persecution of Christians comes through various means. Sometimes the believers' families reject them; sometimes they are attacked along the byway or at night; and sometimes they are imprisoned and tortured—or even killed. Church buildings and homes are frequently burned or destroyed, leaving already destitute believers with nowhere to turn.

But we have the means to help. As Americans, we would never dream of sending our troops unarmed into enemy territory. Likewise, we should not expect these soldiers of God to fight against the forces of darkness in their own countries without the "weapons" to do so. These Kingdom soldiers are our brothers and sisters in Christ, and they need our help. Our responsibility, as believers in the Body of Christ with more resources, is to help those in greater need. To advance the Kingdom of God, we are just as needed as those preaching the gospel on the frontlines. If those of us in industrialized nations mobilized our resources to help native missionaries, the cause of Christ would advance one-hundredfold throughout the world.

> These Kingdom soldiers are our brothers and sisters in Christ, and they need our help.

Today, more than 300,000 native missionaries are preaching the gospel on the frontlines, and they need our support. We cannot let the forces of darkness win. With your help as supply-line soldiers for Christ, Christian Aid can be the modern-day Red Ball Express to help indigenous missions continually advance without retreat.

Practical Ways to Engage Indigenous Missions

Christian Aid Mission serves as a link between donors and indigenous missions so that a witness for our Lord will be established among every tribe, language, and ethnic group in the world. We strive to match the passion and call of the donor with the specific work and focus of an indigenous agency. Opportunities range from sponsorship of missionaries and needy children to financial support of Bible schools, evangelistic crusades, and relief projects. In addition, our service programs and educational materials make it possible for donors to see, touch, and experience missions for themselves.

Together, we can finish the task and reach the unreached around the world with the good news of Jesus Christ.

Ways to Participate

Here are a few ways that you can participate in helping native missionaries in need through Christian Aid Mission:

- *Go Tribal.* Experience a week in the life of an indigenous missionary. Christian Aid offers "vision trips" to pastors, Christian leaders, and young-adult groups. Trip participants will walk alongside native missionaries and experience firsthand the joys and challenges of ministry life. Families and children can engage in the program through Go Tribal *Light.* Come to our headquarters in Charlottesville, Virginia, for an educational presentation that will take you on a journey through the history of Christian Aid and how we support the work of indigenous missions around the world.

- *Mission education and mobilization.* To excite churches about the work of native ministries, we offer opportunities for overseas missionaries to share about their work with congregations, Sunday school classes, or Bible study groups. Our staff can assist your congregation with organizing a missions conference or hosting fundraising events to support overseas projects.

- *Children's ministry.* Give the children in your church, school, or home a glimpse into the adventurous world of missions. *Prayerline for Kids* and other resource materials are available to encourage youngsters to take an active role in supporting indigenous ministries.

Ways to Support

The following are a few ways that you can provide support to assist native missionaries in their ministries:

- *Provide funds for missionaries.* More than 200,000 native missionaries have no regular support. If each could receive just $50 per month, it would greatly encourage their hearts and increase their effectiveness.
- *Supply transportation.* Not one missionary in 100 has a motor vehicle. Jeeps cost about $10,000; vans cost $15,000. Christian Aid wants every mission we assist to have at least one vehicle—even if 200 missionaries must share it. Motorbikes can be supplied for about $1,200, and bicycles for $100 each.
- *Help missionaries print or purchase literature.* Bibles still have to be shipped into closed countries so every believer can have one. By providing funds to help missions buy presses and paper, gospel literature of every type can be printed in most undeveloped countries. Bibles cost about $5 each; paper about $5 per 1,000 sheets; and printing presses from $5,000 to $10,000 each.
- *Send support for Bible institutes.* Indigenous missions operate hundreds of missionary training schools with help from Christian Aid. Students and trainees have nothing to pay, so food and lodging must be provided to them. An effective Bible institute with 100 students can operate on about $3,000 per month.
- *Finance evangelistic crusades.* In the former USSR, many gifted evangelists supported by Christian Aid are preaching to crowds of up to 10,000 people every week. Crusades are also being held in other parts of Asia, Latin America, and many countries in Africa. However, these evangelists don't receive offerings, because up to 90 percent of those in attendance are non-Christians. These individuals need $1,000 to finance a week of meetings with 2,000 in attendance, and $2,000 to reach 5,000 daily.
- *Furnish funds for meeting halls.* Millions of local assemblies gather in tiny one-room houses. When their numbers increase to 100 or 1,000, they have to meet outside, even if it's raining. These congregations would gladly donate the labor to build a meeting

hall, but they have no money to purchase necessary materials such as lumber, bricks, cement, roofing, and windows. About $2,000 will provide a building for 100 believers; $3,000 for 200; or $5,000 for 500.

- *Help ministries care for homeless children.* Most missionary ministries in poorer countries are surrounded by helpless, pitiful widows and orphans on the brink of starvation. These ministries can't just send them all away. The love of Christ constrains them to share with those in need, but they soon run out of food. You can help with gifts of love sent through Christian Aid.

The number one missionary opportunity for God's people in the United States is to be a supply line for indigenous evangelistic ministries in Asia, Africa, Latin America, and Eastern Europe. Send your gifts and offerings through Christian Aid to reach the harvest fields of this needy world in obedience to our Lord's command.

> The number one missionary opportunity for God's people in the United States is to be a supply line for indigenous evangelistic ministries.

To learn more about how you can engage in missions, tear out and send the postage-paid card bound in this book. If the card is missing write to:

Christian Aid Mission
PO Box 9037
Charlottesville, VA 22906
OR contact us:
Phone: 434-977-5650
E-mail: info@christianaid.org
Online: www.christianaid.org

Appendix A

CAN WE REALLY TRUST INDIGENOUS MISSIONS?
By Bob Finley

Those who oppose supporting the work of independent indigenous missions often refer to three stereotypes to validate their arguments:

1. You Can't Trust the "Nationals" with Handling Money

About forty years ago, the head of a traditional mission said to me, "After 100 years of working in Africa, we still have no African we can trust with handling money." I told him that the same would be true if they worked there another 100 years.

Foreign missionaries appeared to be fabulously rich to poor Africans, and their presence caused covetousness among the Africans. The missionaries hired many of the locals to be their servants, often paying them no more than ten cents per day plus food. So, as might be expected, these pitifully poor but intelligent employees were continually seeking some way to trick the rich foreigners and tap into their fabulous wealth.

Indigenous mission leaders are just the opposite. They live on the same level as those within their mission. They are equally poor. They are accountable to one another. If any of them were to try to take too much for themselves, the others would put them out. In general, we have found the leaders of indigenous ministries to be every bit as trustworthy as the heads of missionary organizations based in industrialized countries.

> If any of them were to try to take too much for themselves, the others would put them out.

For example, I once visited a mission based in Nigeria that had about 500 missionaries. Every month, the twenty-four elders of that mission met for a day of prayer. They reviewed an accounting of funds received from all sources that month, and then they prayed for God's guidance as to how all should be distributed, based on the needs of every missionary. I don't know of any mission in the United States that has a more honest and godly way of handling funds that have been entrusted to them.

2. Foreign Support Causes Dependency

There was a time when foreign missionaries went out and set up affiliated churches in poorer countries. These were usually patterned after those at home—large buildings with brick walls, tile or metal roofs, wood or concrete floors, chairs or benches, glass windows, piano or organ, and paid clergy. Impoverished people could not possibly pay for or maintain such institutions, so the missionaries had to subsidize them. The result was dependency.

This process was similar to taking a palm tree from Puerto Rico and transplanting it in Pennsylvania. Survival was possible only in a greenhouse. However, truly indigenous churches are completely different. They have no paid clergy and usually meet sitting on the floor of simple sheds with thatch roofs.

When foreign organizations directly support pastors and churches in poorer countries, it can cause jealousies to arise, divisions to occur, workers to become materialistic, and church members to become irresponsible. Christian Aid avoids creating dependency by never sending funds directly to individuals. Instead, all monies received are sent to responsible native mission boards who distribute it to each missionary.

However, those native missions are not wholly dependent on support from Christian Aid. They were on the job before Christian Aid began helping them, and they would continue their work if our support were cut off. Our help greatly multiplies their effectiveness and spurs rapid growth, but none are totally dependent on that support to carry on the work among their own people.

> Native missions are not wholly dependent on support from Christian Aid. They were on the job before Christian Aid

That's why it is so important to make a distinction between local churches and mission boards. Churches are self-sustaining, but para-church mission boards and other ministries must seek support wherever they can find it among God's people, whether that is at home or abroad.

3. If We Send Money to "Nationals," It Will Corrupt Them

This objection is a half-truth. I have known American missionaries who were good at raising money and worked independently. That is, their finances were not under the strict supervision of a mission board. All the funds they raised went into their personal bank and brokerage accounts. "Trips to the field" were really just vacation jaunts, during which times they stayed with their families in expensive hotels. But to imply that all American missionaries are like that would not be true.

Most missionaries are conscientious in handling funds. Likewise, there may be an occasional individual in a poor country who learns how to raise money abroad and uses it for personal advantage. But these are the rare exceptions. Probably 99 percent of the leaders of indigenous missions handle funds in a responsible manner and are just as accountable as are the heads of mission boards in the United States.

Here again, it is imperative that we emphasize the importance of never sending support directly to individual workers in poorer countries. Christian Aid sends support only to well-established mission groups that keep careful financial records and are fully accountable for all funds received.

> Christian Aid sends support only to well-established mission groups that keep careful financial records

Discover More!

Follow our blog online.
www.christianaid.org/ftt/a

WORLD

Appendix B

A BIBLICAL MOTIVATION IN MISSIONS
By Bob Finley

At most missionary conferences, the theme is likely to be centered on how many human souls are lost in darkness with no hope of salvation. Those who attend are urged, therefore, to "rescue the perishing."

But should that be our main motivation in foreign missions? Surely we should be burdened and concerned for the lost. God is not willing that any should perish (see 2 Peter 3:9). He would like for all men to be saved (see 1 Timothy 2:4). He loved us and gave Himself for us to redeem us from eternal death. So we should likewise love the lost and give ourselves to save them.

But that's not the main purpose of foreign missions as given in the New Testament.

Winning lost souls to Christ is called "evangelism." Every member of every church should be involved in some way in helping spread the good news to every creature. We should realize that all men are sinners in need of a Savior and that without Christ they will be lost forever.

But if this is our only motivation in missions, there is no need to go to foreign countries. Millions of unsaved souls are all around us—and who is to say that the lost in Lhasa are more precious than the lost in Louisville?

A frequent answer is that the lost in Kentucky have a chance to hear the gospel, while millions in Tibet have not had a chance because that land has never admitted foreign missionaries.

In the Word of God, concern for overseas missions is quite different. It centers in the word "apostleship." Paul told the saints in Rome that he had received grace and apostleship for obedience to the faith among all nations, for His name (see Romans 1:5).

That's why Paul had to preach the gospel where Christ was not "named," or "known" (Romans 15:20). Then he said, "But now ... there is no more place for me to [do missionary] work in these regions" (Romans 15:23, NIV). How could he say such a thing? Thousands of lost souls who had never heard the gospel were all around him. Yet he said, "There is no more work for me to do here."

Obviously, Paul's motivation was not just the salvation of souls but also planting churches to honor the name of our blessed Savior where His name had not been known.

When God Almighty looks down on this planet, He seeks a response from the people He has created in His own image. Most have turned to idolatry and are preoccupied with created things rather than their Creator. Covetousness—the desire for earthly things or recognition—is as much idolatry as is bowing to a Buddha (see Colossians 3:5).

Because of idolatry, God confused the people's languages at the tower of Babel and created the nations. When He scattered them to the ends of the earth, He gave them up temporarily (see Romans 1:21–25). In Isaiah 54, the prophet tells how the Messiah will re-gather them (see Galatians 4:27).

That's why God called Abram and promised that through one—and only one (see Galatians 3:16)—of his descendants would all nations be blessed. Until the Messiah came, God's witness on earth was limited to one nation. Looking down from the heavens, He could say, "My house sits in Jerusalem. There I have a people for my name" (see 2 Chronicles 6:6).

But that was temporary, until the Seed—through whom some from every nation would be redeemed—came into the world. When He died for our sins and rose again, the time was fulfilled. Again and again our Lord repeated, "all nations ... all nations."

This was not so that every nation would be converted or Christianized. Just the opposite. Jesus told His disciples that all nations would hate them (see Matthew 24:9). His purpose was to have a witness for Himself, a people for His name, in every nation.

That's why the believers at the first church conference emphasized how our Lord was visiting the nations to take out a people for His name (see Acts 15:14). The original word for church is *ecclesia*, meaning "called out." God had called out some from every tongue, tribe, and nation.

So, the purpose of foreign missions is to build the Lord's house (made of living stones—see 1 Peter 2:5) among those people and in those places where as yet He has no people for His name.

Christian Aid gives priority to helping indigenous ministries in pioneer areas such as Nepal, Bhutan, Sikkim, and Tibet, where the population is unreached for Christ. It supports missionaries such as Prem Pradhan, who found Christ in India and was the only believer in his country of Nepal when he returned there. Not one Christian could be found in the some 100 nations (ethnic groups) located there.

Now, just sixty years later, our Lord has a people for His name among every nation in Nepal. And Prem's disciples, with help from Christian Aid, have been working day and night to build the temple of God among the people (see 1 Corinthians 3:16). Other native missionaries are planting churches among an additional 4,000 ethnic language groups scattered across the earth.

People ask, "If you have contact with 4,000 indigenous ministries comprising more than 200,000 missionaries, how do you know which ones to help?" The answer is simple. We give priority to those who work among unreached people groups. We search out those who go where no Christian has ever gone before. We want to help God's servants in lands where missionaries from America cannot go.

When our Savior spoke of His return to this earth, He told us that He would come again when He has a witness for Himself—a people for His name in every nation (see Matthew 24:14; Mark 13:10).

Even so, come, Lord Jesus.

Discover More!

Connect with us on Twitter to continue the conversation.

twitter.com/christianaid53

Indigenous missions carry on where
Americans are no longer allowed to go as missionaries.

Order the Free Book
Reformation in Foreign Missions

www.christianaid.org/ftt/rfm